ASIAN DILEMMA:

United States, Japan and China

A SPECIAL REPORT FROM
THE CENTER FOR THE STUDY
OF DEMOCRATIC INSTITUTIONS

EDITED BY ELAINE H. BURNELL

PUBLISHED BY
THE CENTER FOR THE STUDY
OF DEMOCRATIC INSTITUTIONS
SANTA BARBARA, CALIFORNIA

At the instigation of prominent members of the Japanese Diet who belong to a special study group of the majority Liberal Democratic Party, the Center for the Study of Democratic Institutions arranged a two-day conference on China policy with their opposite numbers presently, or recently, in the United States government. AMBASSADOR CHESTER RONNING of Canada attended as an observer. The report that follows is a distillation of position papers prepared by the participants and of the transcribed record of six protracted working sessions. SENATOR EDWARD M. KENNEDY of Massachusetts, who had to cancel his attendance, prepared a position paper from which pertinent passages are quoted. These Fellows and Consultants of the Center also participated, and their remarks appear in the transcript: ROBERT M. HUTCHINS, President; HARRY S. ASHMORE, Executive Vice-President; ELISABETH MANN BORGESE, STANLEY SHEINBAUM, and HARVEY WHEELER, Fellows; and HARROP FREEMAN and FRED WARNER NEAL, Consultants.

WILLIAM O. DOUGLAS, an Associate Justice of the U.S. Supreme Court since 1939 and Chairman of the Board of the Center for the Study of Democratic Institutions, was born in 1898. He attended Whitman College, Columbia University, Wesleyan University, and Washington and Jefferson College. He has taught at Yale and Columbia University. He has traveled in Asia, Africa, Europe, and Latin America. His books include *We, the Judges, The Right of the People,* and *America Challenged.*

AIICHIRO FUJIYAMA, head of the Japanese delegation, was born in Tokyo in 1897 and attended Keio Gijuku University. He was President of the Tokyo and the Japan Chamber of Commerce and Industry in 1938. He was first elected to the House of Representatives in 1953. He was Minister of Foreign Affairs from 1957-1959, has twice been Director-General of the Economic Planning Agency, and in 1963 was Chairman of the Executive Council of the Liberal Democratic Party.

MUNENORI AKAGI, from Ibaragi Prefecture, graduated from Tokyo Imperial University in 1927. Experienced in private agriculture and industry, he served twice as Minister of Agriculture and Forestry, once in 1957 and again in 1963-64. His posts in the Liberal Democratic Party include Chief Cabinet Secretary, Chairman of the Research Board, and Chairman of the Executive Board. He has visited mainland China, Europe, the Soviet Union, North, Central, and South America, and Southeast Asia.

MASUMI EZAKI, from Aichi Prefecture, was born in 1922 and graduated from Nippon University. He was elected to the House of Representatives in 1946 and has been reëlected eight times. He has served as Vice-Minister of Construction, Chairman of the Committee on Budget, and Director-General of the National Defense Agency and has occupied a number of positions within the Liberal Democratic Party. He is President of Imasen Electric Company and President of Ichinomiya Women's College.

ICHITARO IDE, Chairman of the Committee on Budget in the Japanese House of Representatives, was born in Nagano Prefecture in 1912. He graduated from the Imperial University in Kyoto and was elected to the House of Representatives in 1946. Since then he has been returned to the Diet ten times. He has been Chairman of the House Committee on Agriculture and Forestry. A member of the Liberal Democratic Party, he was Vice-Chairman of its Foreign Policy Committee.

JOHN SHERMAN COOPER was born in Somerset, Kentucky, in 1901. Graduated from Yale University in 1923, he holds the degree of LL.D. from Harvard University Law School. First elected to Congress in 1946, he has served as United States Ambassador-at-Large, as Ambassador to India and Nepal, as a delegate to the U.N. General Assembly, and as a Congressional adviser to UNESCO. A Republican, he is the senior Senator from Kentucky and a member of the Senate Foreign Relations Committee.

ALAN CRANSTON, born in Palo Alto, California, in 1915, graduated from Stanford University in 1936. He served as a correspondent for International News Service until 1940. He worked to take Italians living in the United States off the enemy-alien list prior to the American invasion of Italy during World War II. A Democrat, he was elected State Controller in 1958 and reëlected in 1962. In 1968 he entered the United States Senate. His book, *The Killing of the Peace,* was published in 1945.

DON EDWARDS, who was born in San Jose, California, in 1915, represents the Ninth Congressional District of California in the House of Representatives. He is a Democrat. He received a bachelor of arts degree from Stanford University, and subsequently he attended Stanford Law School. During 1940 and 1941 he was an agent for the Federal Bureau of Investigation. In addition to serving in the Congress, he was National Chairman of Americans for Democratic Action from 1965 to 1967.

SHUJI KURAUCHI, Director of the House Committee on Foreign Affairs, was born in Fukuoka Prefecture in 1918. After graduating from Tokyo Imperial University in 1942 and serving in the Japanese Army during the Second World War, he joined the staff of the newspaper, *Nishi-Nihon Shimbun*. He was first elected to the House of Representatives in 1958 and has since been reëlected twice. He has served as Vice-Minister of Labor and Vice-Minister of Foreign Affairs.

YASUMI KUROGANE, elected eight times to the House of Representatives since 1952, was born in Yamagata Prefecture in 1910. A graduate of the Imperial University in Tokyo, he entered the Finance Ministry in 1935. He has been a Vice-Minister of the Local Autonomy Agency, Director of the Cabinet Secretariat, and Special Japanese Ambassador to the Tanganyika Independence Ceremony. He is currently Chairman of the Tax System Research Committee of the Liberal Democratic Party.

SHUNICHI MATSUMOTO was born in Hiroshima Prefecture in 1897 and graduated from the Imperial University in Tokyo in 1921. He has served as Ambassador Plenipotentiary to Indochina and to the Court of St. James and as Special Ambassador to South Vietnam, Laos, and Cambodia. Elected to the House of Representatives for the first time in 1955, he has been reëlected twice. In 1961, 1962, 1963, and 1964, he was a member of Japanese delegations to the People's Republic of China.

J.W. FULBRIGHT, senior Senator from Arkansas and Chairman of the Senate Foreign Relations Committee, was born in Sumner, Missouri, in 1905. He holds an A.B. from the University of Arkansas, an A.B. and an M.A. from Oxford University, and an LL.D. from George Washington University. He was elected to Congress in 1943 after serving as President of the University of Arkansas. Among his publications are *Prospects for the West, Old Myths and New Realities,* and *The Arrogance of Power.*

ARTHUR GOLDBERG, born in Chicago, Illinois, in 1908 and a graduate of Northwestern University, was admitted to the Illinois bar in 1929 and the U.S. Supreme Court bar in 1937. He served as General Counsel to the C.I.O., the United Steelworkers, and the A.F.L.-C.I.O. After one year as Secretary of Labor, he was appointed to the U.S. Supreme Court in 1962. He served as Ambassador to the United Nations from 1965-1968. He is the author of *AFL-CIO: Labor United* and *Defenses of Freedom.*

MARK O. HATFIELD, SR., was born in Dallas, Oregon, in 1922. Graduated from Willamette University, he holds a master's from Stanford University. He taught political science at Willamette and was Dean of Students there from 1950-1956. After a number of years in the State Senate, he became Governor of Oregon in 1959. A Republican, he was elected to the United States Senate in 1967 and is now senior Senator from Oregon. His book, *Not Quite So Simple,* was published in 1968.

KAZUO SHIONOYA was born in Shizuoka Prefecture in 1920 and graduated from Waseda University in 1944. At one time he was a member of the Board of Education of Shizuoka Prefecture and head of the Planning Department of Shizuoka Prefectural Office. He was elected to the House of Representatives for the first time in 1966. A member of the Liberal Democratic Party, he is at present a member of the House Committee on Cabinet and the House Committee on Commerce and Industry.

RYOHEI TAMURA, a political scientist, was born in Kochi Prefecture in 1917. He graduated from Waseda University in Tokyo. He was elected five consecutive times to the local Kochi Prefectural Assembly before he ran for the House of Representatives for the first time in 1963. He has been reëlected once since then. A member of the Liberal Party, he is a member of the House of Representatives Committee on Construction and the House Committee on Industrial Public Hazards.

TOKUMA UTSUNOMIYA, a member of the House of Representatives since 1952 and a Liberal Democrat, is President of the 1969 Japan Industrial Exhibition in Peking and Shanghai and Vice-President of the Association for the Promotion of International Trade. Born in Tokyo in 1906, he attended the Imperial University in Kyoto. He has been Vice-Director-General of the Administrative Management Agency and Chairman of the Committee on Discipline. Since 1959, he has made five trips to China.

EDWIN O. REISCHAUER was born in Tokyo in 1910 and educated at Oberlin College and Harvard University. He studied in France, Japan, and China on a Fellowship from the Harvard-Yenching Institute. He has served in the War Department, the United States Army, and the Department of State. Appointed Ambassador to Japan in 1961, he returned to Harvard in 1966. His books include *Japan Past and Present, The United States and Japan, Wanted: An Asian Policy,* and *Beyond Vietnam.*

CHESTER A. RONNING, born in Francheng Hupeh, China, in 1894, entered the Canadian foreign service after earning his A.B. and M.A. from the University of Alberta. He served as Counselor at the Embassy in Chungking and Nanking and as Chargé d'Affaires in Nanking from 1949-1951. He was appointed Director for Eastern Affairs in 1951 and Ambassador to Norway and Minister to Iceland in 1954. He served as High Commissioner to India in 1957 and later in the Legislative Assembly of Alberta.

ELAINE H. BURNELL was born in Shanghai, China, and lived in China and Japan for seventeen years. She was graduated from Smith College with high honors in history and was selected for the Naval Japanese Language Postgraduate School at the University of Colorado. During World War II, she was a WAVE officer assigned to Naval Intelligence. She has been an historical researcher for *Encyclopaedia Britannica* and was later an editor and positions analyst at the Library of Congress.

CONTENTS

PREFACE   Elaine H. Burnell   *xv*

I   AN ISOLATED CHINA: 1
    THREAT TO WORLD PEACE

        1 THE THREE TEACHERS OF   7
           MAO TSE-TUNG

        2 THE INFLUENCE OF UNITED STATES   21
           CHINA POLICY ON SINO-SOVIET AND
           SOVIET-AMERICAN RELATIONS

        3 BARRIERS TO STABILITY AND   27
           PROSPERITY IN ASIA

           Tragic Triangle in Asia:
           Nationalism, Misery, and
           Destitution

           The Need for Imaginative Solutions
           to Asia's Prosaic Problems

II THE MAKING OF AN IMPASSE   37

        4 THE UNITED STATES AND CHINA,   45
           1945 TO 1969

           American Attitudes,
           Past and Present

           The Congress and
           American Asian Policy

           The Power of an American
           President

5 JAPAN'S CHANGING FOCUS 67

6 THE AGGRESSIVE PEOPLE'S REPUBLIC 79
OF CHINA: MENACE OR MYTH?

7 THE VIETNAM WAR IN PERSPECTIVE 91

III THE CRITICAL QUESTIONS: A TIME 103
FOR ENTRENCHMENT OR AN
OPPORTUNITY FOR MODIFICATION?

8 SECURITY FOR EAST AND WEST 109

9 RECOGNITION OF COMMUNIST CHINA: 133
POINTS FOR CONSIDERATION

10 TAIWAN 143

The Pitfalls and Contradictions in
Japan's Taiwan-China Policies

The Two Faces of Formosa:
Model of Progress
and Symbol of Stagnation

11 CHINESE REPRESENTATION IN 155
THE UNITED NATIONS

Communist Chinese Membership:
A First Step Toward World Peace

A Two-China Policy for the
United States

The Value of a United States
Initiative

A Possible Role for the
United Nations

IV A NEW AGE FOR ASIA   175

    12 TRADE AND DEVELOPMENT: 181
       KEYS TO ASIAN STABILITY

    13 THE IMPORTANCE OF   197
       CULTURAL EXCHANGE

    14 THE PROSPECTS FOR THE FUTURE   203

    15 FRESH APPROACHES TO   215
       ANCIENT PROBLEMS

    A New Realism for an
    Outworn Rationality

    Asiatic Union

    Recipe for Survival: An Untried
    Approach in an Unprecedented Age

    Appendix No. I   231
    Appendix No. II   232
    Appendix No. III   233

ACKNOWLEDGEMENTS   238

While traveling in Japan in the spring of 1968, Harrop A. Freeman, Professor of Law at Cornell University and a Consultant to the Center for the Study of Democratic Institutions, called on acquaintances made in the course of his work with the Friends Service Committee. Out of these contacts came a meeting with Tokuma Utsunomiya, Member of the House of Representatives of the Japanese Diet and leader of a study group of the majority Liberal Democratic Party. Mr. Utsunomiya expressed concern over Japanese policy towards China and the conviction that Japan's policy was irrevocably locked to that of the United States.

In a subsequent visit to the United States, Mr. Utsunomiya, whose opinion had been reinforced by talks at the official level in Washington, suggested that he and his colleagues might usefully review the basic questions cf China policy with their opposite numbers from the United States government. Freeman brought the proposal to the Center, which agreed to use its offices to arrange such a conference in January, 1969.

Those present shared one basic conviction: that the time had come for a fundamental change in American and Japanese foreign policy toward the People's Republic of China. In the election of President Nixon, they had read a verdict of the American public expressing dissatisfaction with the Johnson Administration's course in Vietnam. They had seen the policy of isolating China gradually relaxed; now they recognized the need for revision in the policy of containment.

The meetings at Santa Barbara brought forth no quick solutions. The participants tried to bring into focus questions of policy that will affect the United States, Japan, and China in the years to come. To this end, they examined both history and current events. They accepted the fact of Peking's current hostility as inevitable in any country living in isolation, whether isolation be enforced from without or self-inflicted. They did not beg the fact that the prevailing Cultural Revolution in China fosters, and attracts in turn, suspicion and hatred, threatening world peace. But unanimously they challenged the concept of China as an aggressive threat to her neighbors, to Japan, or to the United States. They questioned the wisdom and the practicality of trying to contain a great power whose record of action recently has displayed neither the capacity nor the ambition for conquest.

The end of the Vietnam War, as the participants saw it, would signal the opening of a new epoch in Asia. The policy of isolation had failed; the policy of containment was already in doubt. The advent of this new era would raise new questions concerning the international status of Taiwan, the disposition of military forces in the Pacific, and the role of each of the great powers in Asia. Beyond the immediate difficulties were the demands of the future in an age of increasingly lethal weapons and consequent balance-of-terror diplomacy.

No consensus was sought and none was reached. The aim was to discover the dimensions of the problems that will confront the nations on all sides of the Pacific. Every participant agreed on the fundamental objective: the resolution of international difficulties in Asia without reliance on the force of arms. On the ways and means of approaching the ultimate goal, they disagreed.

This volume reflects the ideas voiced at the conference and set forth in position papers by the participants. These appear, not in the actual sequence in which they were expressed, but in a topical arrangement familiar to all Americans and Japanese concerned with the problems of Asia, present and future. While the participants have cleared their own remarks as they appear here, they have no responsibility for the selection and arrangement of the material; the emphasis and possible bias is that of the editor, who also wrote the italicized introductory passages at the beginning of each of the sections.

ELAINE H. BURNELL

Santa Barbara, California
September, 1969

AN ISOLATED CHINA: THREAT TO WORLD PEACE

"Taking the long view, we simply cannot afford to leave China forever outside the family of nations, there to nurture its fantasies, cherish its hates, and threaten its neighbors."
Richard M. Nixon

China has a tradition of unity, but she has also an unbroken tradition of autocracy in government. Western democratic concepts find little to nourish them in China's heritage. Chinese society, from the family unit to the highest echelons of the government, has for centuries been fundamentally authoritarian.

In the Western Han period, from 206 B.C. to 8 A.D., the character of the traditional Chinese state took form. The Han emperors combined the strict Legalism of the earlier Ch'in period with Taoism and Confucianism to create an ideological and practical base for their authoritarian rule. Taoism, with its stress on passivism and "live and let live," complemented legalistic control.

Confucianism, molded and adapted to meet the needs of the state, gave moral sanction to autocracy. Confucius' theory of human relationships stressed the reciprocal obligations of the emperor and his subjects, but by the thirteenth century Neo-Confucianism was emphasizing the obligation of the inferior to give obedience and loyalty to the superior.

From ancient times the unity of the Chinese state has centered on the person of the emperor. Emperor-worship has had its counterpart in modern times in the cult of Sun Yat-sen, characterized after his death by special weekly memorial observations. The Nationalist Government, during its twenty-two years of mainland rule, continued the tradition in practice, if not in theory. The policy-making power was concentrated in the hands of Chiang Kai-shek, and the spirit of his regime followed the philosophy of ancient imperial rule. Each period of Chinese history has had its charismatic leader, the latest of whom is Mao Tse-tung.

Chinese governmental tradition and Chinese ideology, both ancient and modern, have denigrated the individual. The term "people," in the Chinese sense, is synonymous with the masses, and the Western concept of the individual citizen with his inalienable rights has no parallel in Chinese social and political philosophy. Law in traditional China, while it has been highly developed and rigorously systematized, has always remained the tool of government rather than the guardian of the individual against the abuses of authority. Similarly, the concept of property rights, hallowed in Western minds, is only poorly understood in China.

Obvious parallels may be drawn between Confucian belief in the perfectability of human nature and Communist China's emphasis on education as the means to spiritual rejuvenation. Confucius' famous dictum, "In education there can be no class distinctions," expressed his belief not in the equality *of men but in their* inequality *and was stimulated by a need to bring superior ability into government service. Modern China has come close to realizing the Confucian educational ideal, bringing to bear on the educational system all the psychological and organizational pressures needed to win support for the social system and the state.*

Chinese political and social history, and traditional Chinese ideology, have prepared the way for modern Marxist-Leninist authoritarian rule. The absolutist tradition remains unbroken, notwithstanding the modern deviation from benevolent paternalism and the substitution of communist moral and spiritual values. Marxism-Leninism is the single foreign ideology to find the soil of China congenial. In the hospitable environment provided by two thousand years of authoritarian rule, the communist regime took root, its special forms and patterns of growth determined by twentieth-century pressures and events.

"New China has had three teachers.
"The first teacher was the corrupt politicians of the old China . .
"The second teacher was Japanese militarism . . . .
"The third teacher is American imperialism . . . . "
Chou En-lai

1

The Three Teachers
of Mao Tse-Tung

A STATEMENT BY
Tokuma Utsunomiya

COMMENTS BY:

J. W. Fulbright
Edwin O. Reischauer
William O. Douglas

"If the politicians of the old China had been upright and honest, China would not have taken the course she did, and a New China might not have been born."
Chou En-lai

TOKUMA UTSUNOMIYA:

In 1949 Chiang Kai-shek lost his struggle for power with Mao Tse-tung on the continent of China. He blames his defeat on the diabolical character of Mao's Communist Party and on United States indulgence toward communism at the time. The facts do not bear out Chiang's claims.

During the long rule of the Ming Dynasty and under the early emperors of the succeeding Ch'ing Dynasty, China had been strong and unified. Although it had been an absolute feudal monarchy, its government had been efficient and its armies powerful. Gradually weakened by a rising population, diminished production, emigration, and the waning authority of the emperors, China degenerated into a semi-colonial state after the Nanking Treaty of 1842, which ended the Opium War. The unity of China as a nation was completely destroyed by the rise of local warlords, who partitioned the nation into their private kingdoms, and by the intrusion of foreign nations, who sought to extend their respective spheres of influence through a series of international concessions and settlements. Even at the height of his power, Generalissimo Chiang Kai-shek succeeded in extending his control only to some seven or eight provinces in north and central China. The rest of the twenty-odd Chinese provinces enjoyed a semi-independent status.

After the Japanese invasion of China and during its subsequent struggle with the communists, the Nationalist Government received massive financial support from the United States. During World War II, the United States provided Chiang Kai-shek with well over a billion dollars' worth of materials and military aid; it poured another two billion dollars into the Chinese Nationalist cause from the end of the war until 1948. Even the Soviet Union, under its Treaty of Friendship and Alliance with the Nationalist Government signed on August 14, 1945, promised to provide military aid only to "the Chinese Nationalist Government, which is the Central Government of China." Without question, therefore, the equipment of the Chinese Nationalist forces was incomparably superior to that of the communist troops.

The Kuomintang government fell from the weight of its own corruption and ineptness. The better-equipped and numerically overwhelming troops of Chiang Kai-shek suffered one devastating defeat after another at the hands of the communists. Illustrative is the battle that took place around Yenan in 1947. Nationalist General Hu Tsung-nam, commanding 220,000 troops equipped with the most modern and most powerful arms, occupied Yenan and drove Mao Tse-tung and twenty-thousand of his followers into the mountains to the northeast. There followed two months of mountain warfare during which the superior Kuomintang forces were decimated and, in the end, decisively defeated by Mao's small, ill-equipped band.

In the last analysis, the Nationalist Chinese suffered defeat throughout China because they could not maintain troop morale and failed to win the support of the people. Chiang Kai-shek lost the power struggle for control of China through his own shortcomings as a leader. Paradoxically, the man thus responsible for allowing the communization of China is revered by many Americans and Japanese as an anti-communist hero.

New China must be understood not only as a communist country but also as the first unified and independent nation of Han peoples in many centuries. As a consequence, she has a keen consciousness of her sovereignty and independence. Mao Tse-tung has been able to place the three northeast and various southern provinces, as well as Sinkiang, Inner Mongolia, and Tibet, completely under his control. He has denied the Soviet Union the right to lease Port Arthur and Dairen and terminated other post-World-War-II concessions through which the U.S.S.R. expected to extend its sphere of influence. He has limited foreign control to the small seaport areas of Hong Kong, Kowloon, and Macao.

Unlike the previous government, New China has not ignored the problems of her people. When Mao Tse-tung took over China, this vast land lay wasted and devastated as a result of a hundred years of war, inefficiency, and corruption. Mountains were denuded, and farmlands lay prey to floods and droughts. New China has devoted her energy to reforestation and to laying the foundations of a sound riparian control system. At the same time, the government is engaged in an extensive irrigation program. The people's communes are one means utilized by the central authorities to concentrate labor power in order to improve agricultural conditions. Since my first visit to China in 1959, I have seen the trees planted under these programs grown bigger and hitherto bald mountains covered with a mantle of green.

In the cities and the rural areas the indescribably filthy and the extremely poor, both characteristic of the old China, have disappeared. Even in times of famine, food necessary to sustain life is distributed by the government, and people are clothed and housed, albeit simply. Public sanitation and medical facilities have vastly improved. The bandits and armed robbers of old China have been eliminated; the embezzlement and malfeasance in both the army and the bureaucracy have been greatly reduced. For those of us who are used to the privileges and luxuries of a free society, life in New China could not by any means be pleasant. However, we must recognize the serious efforts being made by the new government to raise the living standard of seven hundred million people and to modernize a nation where only a few years ago, even under the Nationalist regime, slavery and peonage were still facts of life, especially for minority groups.

J. W. FULBRIGHT:

Since 1949 when a communist regime took power on the mainland of China, the American attitude has been one of unrelenting hostility in most respects. Our unfriendly view of the new regime has been met—it should be noted—by at times an equal, and at times an even greater, measure of hostility on the part of China. We saw communist assumption of power in China not as the result of the sicknesses and frailties of China under the Nationalists but as an extension of the Soviet conquest of central Europe. Communism was then regarded, with considerable justification, as a monolithic movement.

It was thus not surprising that the success of the communists in China, following so closely upon the disturbing events in central Europe immediately after the end of the war, dismayed and alarmed the American people. We were further shocked when, following the North Korean attack on South Korea in June, 1950, Chinese forces intervened in November of that year, bringing us face to face with Chinese soldiers in combat for the first time in our modern history. Although the Cold War had frozen our relations with the Soviet Union by 1950, American and Soviet armies had never fought one another. The first large communist power we were to meet on the battlefield was not the Soviet Union but China.

Despite predictions to the contrary, the communist regime has not only survived but has, according to all reports, provided the Chinese people with better conditions of life than any other modern Chinese government. Peking certainly continues to face many internal problems, but so would any regime confronted with the awesome task of administering a nation of seven to eight hundred million people.

Perhaps, after centuries of Western degradation and fifty years of almost constant revolution, what China needs most of the West is to be left alone for awhile.

> *"If the Japanese army had not committed aggression in all parts of China and had not aroused the national feelings of the Chinese people, the birth of a unified New China would not have been possible."*
> Chou En-lai

TOKUMA UTSUNOMIYA:

Japan's policy toward the continent of China over the past half century has stirred up resentment, hatred, and distrust in the hearts of the Chinese people. When the Japanese militarists first launched their expansionist program in the early nineteen-thirties, they met with considerable resistance from a broad segment of the Japanese people, including intellectuals, journalists and writers, and major elements in the political and financial worlds. Criticism emanated even from within the ranks of the military, particularly from the top levels of the Japanese Navy.

In addition to standard repressive measures, the militarists seized upon the issue of communism to maintain their dominant position in Japanese political life. By branding critics as communists and their ideas as "counter to the national policy," the military succeeded in suppressing liberal and democratic thought. While focusing attention on the serious restrictions that *communism* places on individual freedom, the Japanese militarists marched behind the banner of anti-communism to justify their *own* restrictive measures.

In Japan anti-communism was used as a smoke-screen to cover the irrational expansionist policies of the Japanese militarists. Ironically, Japan's military adventures on the

13

Chinese continent, carried out in the name of a crusade against communism, served only to hasten the birth of Communist China.

At one time Japan recognized a large number of regional governments in China and made a variety of commitments to local warlords. The Japanese military government, for example, recognized the regime of Chang Tso-lin in the northeastern provinces, the Manchoukuo government under Emperor Pu-yi, and later the Tuan Chi-jui regime in Peking, the Wang Ching-wei government in Nanking, and the Wang Kuo-min rule in north China. To each of these regimes Japan made commitments, as the United States has to Chiang Kai-shek, not only to protect her interests but to allay her deep fear of latent Chinese nationalism. Japan's failure in China can be attributed, in part at least, to reactionary policies that antagonized young Chinese patriotic leaders and thwarted China's rising nationalistic aspirations. The policy of the militarists was directly contrary to the practices of Japanese leaders in the early Meiji era when Japan gave asylum and encouragement to leaders of China's Republican revolution.

Many Japanese today have the impression that the United States is a country committed to a course in Asia that can lead only to disaster, even as Japan's course during the nineteen-thirties and forties led to her eventual defeat and humiliation.

Even if America's anti-communist, anti-China policy was originally based on rational considerations, this policy today has come to bear close resemblance to the path the Japanese army pursued in the name of anti-communism. I have noted that the more America's Asian policy loses its rationality and flexibility and the more setbacks it suffers, the more high-handed and emotional it becomes. In this sense also America's present-day policy in Asia resembles that of the Japanese militarists. I cannot but feel it is an extremely dangerous policy. It is dangerous in that it can mean vast American losses in terms of both human lives and American resources; and it is dangerous in that it can involve the Japanese people, whether they wish it or not, since by virtue of their geographic and diplomatic position they cannot escape the effects of United States policy in Asia.

EDWIN O. REISCHAUER:

No one can deny the many similarities between the American involvement in Vietnam in the sixties and the Japanese involvement in China in the thirties, but the situation in America today is fundamentally different from that in Japan before the Second World War. Unlike the Japanese Army and Navy, which refused to accept civil control and allowed their own representatives in the field wide freedom of action, the American military has retained its scrupulous obedience to civilian control and its traditional firm discipline. The mistakes the United States has made in Vietnam are primarily the mistakes of its civilian leaders. The frequent warnings we hear in the United States against the military-industrial complex do not signify fear of a crude takeover of government by military officers, as happened in Japan. They are meant to alert Americans to the undue pressure that military and industrial groups can exert through the normal procedures of bureaucracy and the democratic electoral process.

Unlike Japan, which moved from the already restrictive basis of the Peace Preservation Law of 1925 to the virtual elimination of all expressions of dissident opinion, debate on the Vietnam War in the United States has been entirely free and has become progressively more intense. In basic political structure and public attitudes the United States is very different from prewar Japan.

A sharp shift in its approach, not only toward Vietnam but toward the broader problems of East Asia, is entirely possible and is, I feel, already well under way. The modification I detect in American attitudes is, of course, far from complete and is still to produce a clear change of posture.

"If the American forces had not advanced in Korea to the very borders of our northeast provinces and triggered the Chinese army into action, our socialism would have been more slow-paced in its advance."
Chou En-lai

TOKUMA UTSUNOMIYA:

Until we recognize the strong nationalistic coloring of the newly united Han peoples on the Chinese mainland, we will not understand New China's attitudes toward the United States presence in Asia, her efforts to develop nuclear weapons, or her hostile relations with the Soviet Union. The key to New China's foreign relations is her keen sense of national sovereignty.

When I visited with Prime Minister Chou En-lai in 1961, he made a remark of great significance: "It is not we who have occupied Hawaii or Alaska, but it is the United States that has occupied Taiwan. It is the United States that is the invader and not China." This interpretation of the American role in Taiwan provides a clue to the Chinese meaning when they speak of "American imperialism." For New China, the main problem of Taiwan is not that a government with a different ideology exists there but that in Taiwan the sovereignty of New China is denied and the island is "occupied" by a foreign country, the United States.

China and the Soviet Union, as socialist countries, have much in common. A basic difference, however, is that, while the Soviet Union inherited vast territories annexed by Czarist Russia, New China inherited a country eroded by invasions and degraded into semi-colonial status. Fresh in China's memory are the lands preëmpted from China by the Russians through the Treaty of Aigun and the Treaty of Peking. It is fair to say that China's nuclear armament is a manifestation of her desire to be independent from the Soviet Union in coping with America's nuclear threat. The need to escape from reliance on the Soviet nuclear umbrella is consistent with Defense Minister Lin Piao's insistence that China learn to defend herself on her own soil, using the formula of a people's war.

As Chou En-lai indicated to me, the Korean War prompted China's decision to collectivize her farms and nationalize her small and medium enterprises. Later she used the mechanism of the Cultural Revolution to place the entire nation on a wartime footing. I believe that we would be mistaken, however, if we linked these developments and her strong new sense of sovereignty to a policy of expansionism. China has no colonies and has been careful to take no action that would run counter to feelings of nationalism in North Vietnam and North Korea. New China's basic attitude on territorial questions, I believe, can be explained in terms of her desire to demarcate and stabilize her frontiers as they were during the last years of the Ch'ing Dynasty. Seen in this light, her persistent demands for the return of Taiwan, her insistence on the recognition of traditional boundary lines along the Sino-Indian border, and her worsening relations with the Soviet Union become rational responses, the understandable attitudes of a nation seeking to ward off threats to her newfound independence.

WILLIAM O. DOUGLAS:

In the minds of some, the Peking regime has been the real *bête noire* in the Vietnam situation. Many have thought that Peking is inspiring, encouraging, and helping to instigate revolt, rebellion, and insurgence in her rather large zone of interest in Southeast Asia. Our military effort in Vietnam is therefore supposed to tell Peking and any rebellious satellites that violent revolution does not pay.

Peking and Delhi have armies facing each other, and one school of thought favors the West arming India so that her troops can help level the Chinese. This same group pleads with Japan to renounce her constitution, rearm with modern weapons, and make ready to crush the mainland.

With Japan and India rearmed, the encirclement of mainland China would be impressive. The American forces already have a fortress in Vietnam and another in Thailand. We have thirty-five thousand troops aboard warships off the Vietnamese coast, 535,000 in Vietnam, and forty-five thousand in Thailand. Formosa, as one of our military strategists said in the early fifties, is considered a flat-topped carrier within easy striking distance of all the factories of the mainland. We have fifteen thousand troops on Taiwan. In South Korea fifty-five thousand American men stand guard. In Japan, Okinawa, and the Philippines we have 116,000 troops. Over-all, we have about 900,000 troops in Asia and in the near reaches of Asia. And the Seventh Fleet is also a force with which to reckon.

President Johnson always gave great credence to our reliance on force to settle world problems. In speaking to American troops in Korea on November 1, 1966, he said:

There are three billion people in the world, and we have only two hundred million of them. We are outnumbered fifteen to one. If might did make right, they would sweep

18

over the United States and take what we have. We have what they want. . . .

We have had to show it couldn't be done in Korea. We may have to show it can't be done in other areas of the Pacific. We are showing right now it can't be done in Vietnam. . . .

America's orientation, unquestionably, has been military; and the military orientation of the West toward Peking is ominous. At whatever point on the perimeter one examines the Western position vis-à-vis China, the clearer is its military stance. That military stance recreates the image of Japanese militarism that was one of the powerful catalytic agents uniting the Chinese people under a communist flag.

Japan has been a collaborator in the military posture of the West. She recognized Taiwan by the treaty of April 28, 1952, a step taken under American pressure. The United States-Japan Security Treaty of September 8, 1951, and the Treaty of Mutual Coöperation and Security of January 19, 1960, gave the United States bases in Japan with a view to protecting Japan against "armed attack from without." Those treaties had their main inspiration in fear of Peking. Although Japan has had no expeditionary force on Asia's mainland since the Second World War, she has played an important role in sustaining the American military attitude toward the Peking regime.

To many Americans, their country is not the home of the rich about to be robbed by the poor of the world. In their view, America has a great role to play in a coöperative world structure, contributing her technological and managerial skills to all struggling peoples and helping to establish gentle and simple regimes of law that will take the place of fantastically expensive and utterly destructive regimes of force to settle international disputes.

If we all insist on military solutions to international problems, Peking will in time be a formidable contender. It would, I suppose, be possible to cause the vast energies of the new generation in any nation to explode outwardly and to make subduing the "enemy" a holy cause.

"The way of the peacemaker is even harder than is commonly supposed.

"Responsive, sober Russians believe that at least some of the Americans who want to bring China into the community of nations are actuated not by a desire for peace but by enmity toward the Soviet Union.

"In a paranoid world the way of the peacemaker is hard, indeed."
Robert M. Hutchins

2

The Influence of United States China Policy on Sino-Soviet and Soviet-American Relations

A STATEMENT BY
Fred Warner Neal

THE INFLUENCE OF UNITED STATES CHINA POLICY ON SINO-SOVIET AND SOVIET AMERICAN RELATIONS

FRED WARNER NEAL:

America's estrangement from mainland China is more than a quarrel between two great nations. It is a serious problem for all mankind. In a revolutionary and thermonuclear era, the hostility between the largest and potentially the most powerful state in Asia and the world's most advanced industrial power, if it continues, may well determine the shape of the future or even if there is to be a future. The complicated network of relationships between these two nations and the third nuclear power, the Soviet Union, involves more than just Americans and Chinese, and the issue must stand, therefore, at the head of the agenda for all nations and all peoples.

Yet it is fair to say that the United States has more of a non-policy than a policy on China. Its position is made up of attitudes, fears, and a variety of ad-hoc measures. American non-policy has two remarkable and contradictory characteristics: one is its consistency, or rigidity; the second, its insufficiency. From time to time, American leaders have publicly raised questions about peripheral aspects of our relationship with China, but none has ever suggested fundamental changes. At the same time, however, American officialdom, from the very top to the bottom—with some noteworthy exceptions—has sensed the inadequacy of United States policy (or non-policy) on China. Among scholars concerned with foreign policy and international relations, this feeling is well-nigh universal.

Prominent among the influential groups of Americans arguing strongly for a change in United States policy toward China are those concerned with arms control and disarmament. Their primary and most telling point is that no agreements on thermonuclear weapons, whether aimed at control or abolition, can be meaningful without the participation of China. They see American security constantly jeopardized by the absence of these agreements. They believe that while China today refuses to participate in such negotiations as the test-ban and the non-proliferation treaties, a more coöperative attitude can be expected as China increases her nuclear capacity if her relations with the United States improve meanwhile. The Communist Chinese, as this group points out, have never refused to discuss disarmament as such. At one time, indeed, China did propose—without a response from Washington—a Pacific nuclear-free zone. From the standpoint of disarmament, according to this argument, American policymakers are still prisoners of an outworn attitude: the earlier conviction in Washington that Communist China did not have the capacity for major thermonuclear power, an assumption whose fallacy has been amply demonstrated.

The relationship of China policy to disarmament involves questions of Soviet-Chinese and American-Soviet relations. The deep split within the international communist movement has given rise to speculation on the nature of China's territorial ambitions, if any. One school of thought, represented in some official American circles, anticipates serious border conflicts between the Soviet Union and China. If this view is correct, China can be expected to expand northward toward Soviet territories once Chinese; between her internal preoccupation and the eventuality of armed conflict with the Soviet Union, China could not pose a real threat to the United States. Other experts, among them Professor John King Fairbank of Harvard, feel that Peking has accepted, by and large, the status quo on its north and northwest frontiers and is interested primarily in developments in Southeast Asia.

Whatever the relative merit of these conflicting opinions, the Sino-Soviet split has vastly complicated Washington-Moscow relations. One factor in the hostility between Peking and the Kremlin has been the effort toward détente with the United States initiated by Khrushchev. Khrushchev saw the need for agreements on thermonuclear weapons between the United States and the Soviet Union and recognized the advantage of avoiding military conflict in general. His policy pledged the Soviet Union not to stir up wars of national liberation and downgraded violent revolution as an effective means of spreading socialism. This is essentially the meaning of the new concept of coexistence evolved by the Soviet Union between 1956 and 1962.

The Chinese, while not opposing coexistence as such, are inclined to question its central thesis, that war in the present era is not inevitable and can and must be avoided. Moreover, the détente envisaged by Moscow would probably require an agreement aimed at maintaining the status quo. Nothing would please Communist China less so long as the United States is following a policy of containment. Seeing the United States as her prime threat, Peking apparently believes that only when she has adequate thermonuclear capacity can she deal with the United States as a military equal. Arms control, therefore, is seen at present as against the Chinese interest since it would interfere with China's nuclear development.

While both the Soviet Union and the People's Republic of China have as their immediate aim the spread of socialist ideology, Moscow feels that success depends on avoiding war, something also in the Soviet national interest. Peking, on the other hand, accepts the risk of war as perhaps a necessary corollary to both her national and her ideological interests. In this sense, the Soviet view and the Chinese understanding of the historical process are fundamentally inimical.

Taking this basic philosophical divergence into account, former Senator Joseph Clark of Pennsylvania and Professor Hans Morgenthau of the Center for the Study of American Foreign Policy in Chicago agreed at the Senate Foreign Relations Committee hearings in 1966 that an important ingredient of American policy toward China should be establishing a détente with the Soviet Union. Senator Clark felt that only with a relaxation of strained Soviet-American relations could a realistic containment of Peking come about, not "to crush China but for some sort of sensible accommodation that would restrain the more belligerent tactics and points of view within the Maoist hierarchy." Noting that containment of China by the United States alone is impracticable, Walter Lippmann has declared that such a policy is possible only in collaboration with China's great Asian neighbors, including not only the Soviet Union but also Japan, India, and Pakistan.

The most questionable aspect of the idea of United States-Soviet collaboration to contain China is that it ignores Soviet pretensions to leadership of the communist world. Thus far the U.S.S.R. has bent over backward to avoid any appearance of collusion with the United States against China. Its position of leadership has already suffered, however, from Chinese accusations that Moscow is pursuing narrow national interests at the expense of the higher goals of communism. Even so, should the Sino-Soviet conflict threaten to move toward military confrontation, the kind of collaboration envisaged by Senator Clark might be possible. More important, an improvement in United States-Soviet relations, by contributing immeasurably to world stability, might help create an atmosphere conducive to improved United States-Chinese relations. On the other side of the coin, amelioration of American-Chinese hostility in the absence of a détente with the Soviet Union might result in a deeper cleavage between the United States and the U.S.S.R.

For all these reasons, reconsideration of American China policy is likely to be the most fundamental item on the foreign policy docket of the new Administration in Washington. Basic American attitudes toward the People's Republic of China are inescapably involved in the two matters of greatest urgency in American foreign affairs: the Vietnam War and the clarification of relations with the Soviet Union. With regard to the U.S.S.R., the United States has some general understanding of the issues and has worked out a *modus operandi;* in short, the problems are in focus. But with respect to China, Americans have little clear conception of where they want to go, much less of how to get there.

*"We just want to be free from the terror and
the weapons of soldiers . . .
"We want our children to read, we don't
want them to be sick all their lives and we
want to grow our own food on our own land."*
Vietnamese Village Chief

3   Barriers to Stability and Prosperity in Asia

TRAGIC TRIANGLE IN ASIA: NATIONALISM, MISERY, AND DESTITUTION

A STATEMENT BY
Aiichiro Fujiyama

THE NEED FOR IMAGINATIVE SOLUTIONS TO ASIA'S PROSAIC PROBLEMS

A STATEMENT BY
Yasumi Kurogane

TRAGIC TRIANGLE IN ASIA:
NATIONALISM, MISERY, AND DESTITUTION

AIICHIRO FUJIYAMA:

History has taught us a sad lesson. We could have coped with communism in Asia without fear, without hostility, and without loss of life. We could have provided the people of each emerging country with economic aid, with food, and with the means to work and earn. Instead, we supplied them with arms. The Vietnam problem is the ultimate consequence of our shortsightedness.

It is particularly sad that America's approach to communism in Asia should have become the Achilles' heel of its foreign policy. In the past, the United States has had the cleanest hands of all the Western nations in its international relations. Even during the Second World War the United States made heroic efforts to effect conciliation and collaboration between the Nationalist and the Communist Chinese.

After World War II the countries of Asia, most of them newly independent, struggled with economies impoverished by years of colonial exploitation and the recent fighting. Once freed from colonialism, these nations had three immediate aims: to maintain their independence; to eliminate poverty; and to stabilize their living conditions. It was not surprising, indeed it was inevitable, that many of them sought to achieve their goals by distributing goods in short supply on an egalitarian basis and by enacting political measures designed to provide security to peoples with a long legacy of foreign domination. Had the Western nations helped to improve the livelihood of these Asian peoples, they would have been effective in countering the communist appeal. Instead, by branding Asian efforts at self-improvement as "communist," the advanced countries of the West created deep resentment and drove many nations of Asia into the communist camp. The democracies of the world should reflect upon this most recent lesson of history.

America's entire Asian policy has turned on the containment of Communist China, but the United States has not stopped with containment alone. Assuming that the nations of Asia, like dominoes, would fall one after another before the communist onslaught, the United States hastened to set up governments amenable to its will and attempted to surround China. As a result, America is today in direct confrontation with the People's Republic of China.

Communist propaganda, which capitalizes on social unrest, cannot appeal to the people of an area where just and democratic government exists. Japan is a case in point. As long as Japan enjoys freedom of speech, fair living standards, and the prospect of continued economic development, the large majority of the Japanese people will reject communism as a political system. The establishment of a communist regime in present-day Japan by either indirect aggression or revolution is unthinkable.

This is not to say that Asia can enjoy peace and prosperity under the present circumstances. My father had great wisdom. Even when I was a child, he used to tell me that Japan's future depended on her continued friendly relations with China and with the United States. He made me travel through China while I was still a university student, and he sent my four younger brothers to American prep schools and universities. Had my father's thinking prevailed, Japan might have avoided her tragic prewar course in China; if it prevailed in Japan today, Asian stability would have much brighter prospects.

Japan's relations with China are much more important to her, as an Asian country, than America's relations with China are to the United States. Postwar Japan could have reëstablished friendly contacts with the mainland of China, maintaining at the same time close ties with the United States. Fear of communist infiltration during the serious food shortages of the early postwar years led Japan to align herself with America's containment policy, and because of typically Japanese sympathies for Chiang Kai-shek on Taiwan, Japan lost her immediate chance to reopen the channels of communication with New China.

When we look at mainland China, with her 780,000,000 people and her 9.95 million square kilometers of territory, it is evident that we cannot think of peace, stability, and prosperity for Asia without taking China into consideration. Furthermore, we cannot speak of future progress in the world while we ignore the Chinese people with all their experience in creating one of the world's great cultures over many long years of history.

THE NEED FOR IMAGINATIVE SOLUTIONS
TO ASIA'S PROSAIC PROBLEMS

YASUMI KUROGANE:

The land mass of Asia, lying between the Pacific and the Indian Oceans, is an area where the communist world that revolves around the People's Republic of China confronts the free world countries allied with the United States. As a result, it has great importance both militarily and politically. The world balance of power depends, to a very real extent, on the direction that the nations of this region choose to follow.

The countries that comprise Asia vary widely in race, language, political organization, and societal structure. They lack the cohesiveness implied by the term "Asia." Actually, the interests of Japan, Communist China, the Republic of Korea, Taiwan, and the countries of Southeast Asia do not always coincide. In this area where most countries gained their independence after the Second World War, the pronounced trend is toward increasing nationalism; we can expect disputes to go on erupting between neighboring countries and regional instability to continue for some time into the future.

Furthermore, most Asian countries carry within themselves the elements of political unrest. Inexperience in self-government is only one factor creating internal chaos. Economics plays an important, if not a decisive, role. Japan stands alone as an industrially advanced power in the Western sense. The Republic of Korea, Taiwan, Thailand, and the Philippines have somewhat advanced economies. All the rest—Cambodia, Vietnam, Burma, Indonesia, Laos, and Communist China—are developing countries. They vary in the extent of their growth, but all can be classed as economically backward. Poverty, with its companion, illiteracy, provides the basis for widespread dissatisfaction and prevents the development of politically stable regimes.

In addition, many new Asian countries fear Communist Chinese aggression. Viewed objectively, Chinese aggressive intentions may be more mythical than real, but a stubborn distrust of the communists prevails nonetheless among some Southeast Asians, the inhabitants of Taiwan, and, to a lesser extent, the Japanese.

To complicate matters further, the People's Republic of China, the Soviet Union, the United States, Taiwan, and Japan all have varying degrees of interest in Southeast Asia. Contrary to the usual assumptions, the evidence is that Communist China's major concern in that area is not with inciting revolution or spreading her ideology but with establishing economic ties. While her total trade volume in 1968 was under four billion dollars, China's export surplus in trade with the nations of Southeast Asia exceeded four hundred million dollars, and she has been extending small amounts of economic aid to North Vietnam, Cambodia, and other countries of the region.

Taiwan depends on Japan and the United States for a large

part of both her imports and her exports, but Southeast Asia still accounts for twenty per cent of her total exports. Thus, Taiwan cannot afford indifference to events in Southeast Asia.

The Soviet Union has recently established diplomatic relations with Singapore and Malaysia. Although Soviet interest in Southeast Asia by no means matches her involvement in the Near and Middle East, the U.S.S.R. nevertheless feels that it cannot abandon Southeast Asia to the United States and Communist China.

The United States, as leader of the free world, has no choice but to take a grave interest in Southeast Asia. Peace, security, and prosperity on a global scale could be threatened by any new crisis in that region.

Japan has a special stake in maintaining trade relations with Southeast Asia as well as with the Republic of Korea, Taiwan, and Communist China. Southeast Asia is an important source of raw materials for Japan and a market for Japanese products; trade with this region accounted for thirty-one per cent of Japanese exports in 1967 and twenty-eight per cent of her imports. Protected trade routes are vital to the economic life of an island nation; in particular, disturbances in Southeast Asia can threaten the supply line for Japan's crude-oil imports, nearly half of which come from the Near and Middle East.

To break down the present barriers to stability and prosperity in Asia, what is needed today is not a showdown of force between the free world and the communist world but an elevation in the standard of living for Asia's impoverished peoples. In an area where nationalism is the prevailing force, anti-communism can have only a limited appeal and will automatically bar communist or neutral elements from future regional coöperative movements. The signs today point toward a growing feeling of solidarity among the underdeveloped Asian countries. It is doubtful that this sense of solidarity will lead to new military alliances in Asia; rather, it can be expected to focus on preserving law and order and on the peaceful settlement of recurrent disputes. To foster and expedite coöperation among Asian nations, the existing machinery of the Asia-Pacific Council, the Association of South East Asian Nations, the Cabinet Ministers' Conference on Southeast Asia Development, and perhaps the Economic Commission for Asia and the Far East and the Asian Development Bank, can provide the basic means.

If regional coöperation is to become a reality in Asia, aid from the advanced countries will be essential. Both Japan and the United States provide some assistance at present, but the effort has been small compared to similar programs for Africa and Latin America. In 1967, when her balance of international trade deteriorated, Japan contributed only .93 per cent of her national income to economic and technological aid for her neighbors. Furthermore, United States aid to Asian countries has shown a tendency to decline in recent years.

With a gross national product eight times that of Japan, the United States will, it is hoped, consider the military and political importance of Asia sufficient reason to increase rather than decrease its aid. As Japan's economic growth continues, she can be expected to assume a greater share of the aid burden in her own national interest.

Conditions in Asia dictate that priority should be given to modernizing agricultural methods, developing power sources, and improving transportation and technology. Adequate planning and sustained guidance during the execution of aid programs will assure efficient fund distribution and utilization. In addition, the advanced countries should consider bolstering their aid measures by purchasing the primary products of the developing areas and by allowing preferential tariffs.

When peace is finally restored, both North and South Vietnam will present special problems. Both regions face widespread urban and agricultural devastation as well as the more basic problems of underdevelopment. The stabilization of North Vietnam, in particular, is indispensible to the maintenance of peace in Asia.

As the nations of Asia progress economically, their tendency to squabble among themselves can be expected to decline. In this connection, the United States has an important psychological role to fulfill. A sudden loss of American interest or the immediate pullback of American personnel to the mid-Pacific could exacerbate the anxieties of the little countries of Asia, supplementing fear of communism with distrust of the free world.

The long-range objectives of stability and prosperity in Asia require collaboration between the United States and Japan, in concert with Australia, New Zealand, and Canada. Furthermore, none of these countries can afford to ignore or to antagonize Communist China further. The geographically distant nations of Asia cannot pose an immediate threat to the security of the United States and her allies, but continuing crises in this area can and will threaten the peace and stability of the world at large.

II

THE
MAKING
OF
AN IMPASSE

"All great moves forward in the history of mankind have required changes of existing attitudes and states of mind, so that real life can catch up with the creative ideas that underlie our evolution."
U Thant

For China, the nineteenth century was more than a period of severe humiliation at the hands of the West. It was a time of internal disintegration and social tension. Dynamic currents of Western thought, riding the wave of economic adventurism, infiltrated a society burdened with a decaying dynastic structure and torn by local rivalries. The old China cracked and split under the pressures. From the ruins of the ancient regime, new philosophies and new leaders emerged.

The unity and strength of traditional Chinese civilization had centered on the imperial throne and the personal rule of the emperor. The last years of the Ch'ing dynasty witnessed a decline in the quality of imperial leadership and with it a creeping corruption throughout the empire. The ministers of the court, long the guiding hands of the emperor and a major source of his wisdom, were in the nineteenth century all too often sycophants or symbols of personal corruption. Brigandage and disorder mounted in the countryside, weakening still further the hold of the central government. Secret societies flourished. The White Lotus Rebellion of 1796-1804 and the Taiping and Triad Rebellions in the eighteen-fifties, in which millions died, involved large groups of discontented peasants and landlords alike, presaging major upheavals to come. Equally significant, each of the rebellions was crushed; the old order could still marshal its strength.

For the most part, the discontent manifested in the rebellions did not represent a desire to overturn the traditional order or to liberalize social institutions. Popular uprisings were aimed at governmental corruption and lassitude and, except for the reforms attempted by the Taipings, offered little threat to Confucian and Neo-Confucian philosophies. Although there was some significant change in intellectual and social attitudes in the early part of the nineteenth century, appreciable concern with reform came only after the intrusion of the nations of the West.

Because of the stress modern scholars have placed on the exploitative nature of the Western drive into China, they have tended to pass over the impact of Western ideas on the Chinese with whom Americans and Europeans did business.

With some notable exceptions, Western theory and Western example did not stimulate Chinese merchants and businessmen to advocate a full range of governmental and societal reforms, but a new class of independent bourgeois did emerge in the Western-dominated trading centers. The traders, bankers, and compradores in the port cities gradually dropped old values in favor of a new entrepreneurial spirit. Impressed by Western success, these men developed respect for individualism, in business at least, and adopted with enthusiasm the Western technology and competitive spirit.

The contrast between Western dynamism and Chinese decadence made a deep impression upon intellectuals also. Some few, like K'ang Yu-wei, Ho K'ai, and Hu Li-yuan, advocated sweeping political, economic, and social reforms to bring the monarchy and the people into closer communication and even went so far as to advance the concept of individual equality. Probably the great majority, impressed by Western technology, including its war-making capacity, subscribed to the formula of Chang Chih-tung: "Chinese learning for the essential principles, Western learning for practical applications."

A more familiar result of Western expansion in China was the strengthening of Chinese nationalism. Feelings of cultural superiority had long dominated Chinese thinking, but China's impotence in the face of Western exploitation and effrontery stimulated a new kind of national consciousness that united diverse elements in a fierce desire to return China to a position of wealth and strength. The Western concept of the "Yellow Peril" had its reverse in the "White Peril" the Chinese saw menacing every aspect of their national life. China suffered under a legal and economic double standard imposed by white men to guarantee unobstructed exploitation. Chinese in every walk of life were introduced to Western culture from the perspectives of white racism, white greed, and white arrogance. The White Peril for China was no vague image called up to justify a governmental course. It was a daily stark reality of life, threatening the existence of the world's largest state. Resentment against the West permeated Chinese society, and, significantly, the most brutal, rampaging expressions of anger came from the peasants.

The liberalizing effects of Western political, economic, and social theory, combined with a degenerate dynastic rule and injured national pride, might have brought into being a new centralized state cast in a republican mold had not the authoritarian and divisive tendencies persisted. Sun Yat-sen, in many ways the spiritual father of Mao Tse-tung, briefly set up such a state, based on his Three Principles of Nationalism, Democracy, and People's Livelihood; however, he could not marshal sufficient support, either at home or abroad, to maintain control. A weak China served the interests of the West, and warlordism,

characteristic of the last years of the
Ch'ing, continued to plague China into
the twentieth century.

Chiang Kai-shek, successor to Sun
Yat-sen at the head of the Kuomintang
Party, devoted his considerable energies
to ending military separatism; by ruthless
manipulation and suppression and by
playing for time with the foreign powers
he achieved a considerable degree of
political reintegration. He managed to
temper or eliminate some of the most
abusive foreign concessions and privileges,
but he was unable to thwart Japanese
imperial ambitions. Socially and
politically, his outlook was conservative,
and to the limited extent that he could
reassert central control, he symbolized
only a new authoritarianism in the
pattern of the old.

The Communist leaders who took power
in 1949 grew up in the age of Western
ascendancy in China; their ideas were
molded and shaped by the nation's
humiliation. They saw the magic that
modern technology, particularly
transportation and mass communication,
had worked for the benefit of foreigners.
They learned from the West the power
of a gun and from their own struggles
the potential of an enraged, exploited
peasantry. They were bred in an era of
militarism and of a nationalism the
more intense because it could find no
effective expression. On the tradition of
Chinese unity, reinforced by anti-foreign
feelings, they built a strong, modern,
central regime.

"American foreign policy is often forged in the heat of crisis rather than hammered out with wisdom and foresight.
"It frequently happens, then, that a policy designed to serve a critical circumstance becomes obsolete even as it is being shaped."
Mark O. Hatfield

---

4   The United States and China, 1945 to 1969

AMERICAN ATTITUDES, PAST AND PRESENT

A STATEMENT BY
Fred Warner Neal

THE CONGRESS AND AMERICAN ASIAN POLICY

A STATEMENT BY
John Sherman Cooper

THE POWER OF THE PRESIDENT

A STATEMENT BY
Don Edwards

AMERICAN ATTITUDES, PAST AND PRESENT

FRED WARNER NEAL:

American responses to Communist China have been conditioned by the Chinese civil war in which the United States was an active participant; by the absence of an over-all settlement of World War II; by the revolutionary situation in Asia; and by the current deep split within the international communist movement. Since the Korean War, American China policy has had two objectives, both negative: containment and isolation.

Containment has been pursued through military and politico-economic means, with emphasis on the military. The United States has committed its support to the Republic of China, guaranteeing protection to Taiwan and the offshore islands. It has intervened militarily on the Asian mainland in Korea and Vietnam and has given military and economic support to anti-Chinese Asian governments. It has capped these actions with a series of interlocking treaties, bilateral and multilateral, embracing as much of non-communist Asia as possible; in most cases it has supported the treaties with a substantial American military presence.

Isolation has been pursued via non-recognition, opposition to seating Peking in the United Nations, an embargo on trade, and a policy of discouraging, and often thwarting, cultural contacts.

China sees the twin objectives of American Asian policy as a direct challenge to what may be called her core interests, those she considers vital to her life as a state. All states have core interests, and, even in an era of intercontinental missiles, statesmen disregard the importance of geography at their peril.

For smaller states, defending core interests may amount to no more than preserving territorial integrity. The core interests of larger, more powerful states like China extend, at a minimum, to immediately contiguous areas. Peking perceives American actions in the Pacific as a continuing threat to her very existence; and she is particularly sensitive to the United States policy of non-recognition, involving as it does the fiction that the Taiwan regime is the legitimate government of all China. As a consequence China has, with increasing hostility, enunciated a counter-policy aimed at ending these presumed threats. Her proclaimed goal is the elimination of American influence throughout Asia, her minimal objective the removal of the American military presence from the Asian mainland and adjacent waters.

American postwar foreign policy toward China is illuminated by the history of relations between the two countries since the end of the eighteenth century. Following the initial American trading venture with China in 1784, the primary United States ties with the Eastern colossus were economic. Americans enjoyed from the start the special treatment secured in the so-called unequal treaties; the first American diplomatic accord with China, the Treaty of Wanghia in 1844, dealt with an extension of these privileges. Yet America's role in Chinese affairs very early took a unique turn that distinguished it from the actions of the other "barbarians" and gave it the mixture of economic self-interest and altruism later embodied in the Open Door.

Along with American economic penetration of China came the missionaries. Although never highly successful in their proselyting endeavors, the missionaries did create a special interest and concern about China in the United States, especially in the Protestant churches. A great many Americans first heard of China when asked in Sunday school to contribute their pennies to missionary activities and thus came to feel they had a personal stake in the distant land.

In the latter part of the nineteenth century American influence expanded westward across the Pacific; with the acquisition of the Philippine Islands in 1898, the United States belatedly became a Far Eastern colonial power. Henceforth, the United States would be inextricably involved with power politics in China.

At the turn of the century other Western nations were

stepping up competitive efforts on the Asian mainland. From Washington, this race for power and privilege seemed not only to jeopardize American commercial privileges but also to pose a threat to the Philippines. The United States response, influenced by the British, was to proclaim the policy of the Open Door. It was in many ways typical—a unilateral effort to further American interests stated in altruistic terms.

Exactly what the Open Door policy meant was never clear, except that all powers should have equal commercial opportunities in China. It did not, for example, prompt the United States to respond to Sun Yat-sen's pleas for assistance in modernizing the feudal government, and almost by default the new Chinese republic turned to Soviet Russia for support. Although the policy was embodied in the Washington Nine Power Treaty of 1922, no machinery was provided for implementing its protective features. When Japan made excursions into Manchuria, the United States issued various declarations condemning the intervention but neither extended substantial aid to the Nationalist regime nor curbed its sale of strategic items to Japan; indeed, American trade with Japan played an important part in Japanese military successes on the mainland.

After Pearl Harbor, China became an American ally in the war against Japan. In response to a variety of military and diplomatic pressures, President Roosevelt formulated an Asian policy that made China one of the major allied powers. During and after the war years Generalissimo Chiang Kai-shek and his wife caught the imagination of the American people as heroic figures in the resistance to Axis aggression. In a public relations sense, at least, the idea of China as a great power and close ally became an integral part of the American view of the world.

At the same time, however, the United States was encountering the reality of growing Chinese communist strength. In the campaigns against the Japanese, the United States established liaisons with the communist forces and extended aid to them. This assistance began primarily with a military rationale, but it came to reflect a belief that there was no insoluble conflict between the basic aims of the communists and the Kuomintang.

These wartime relationships hopelessly entangled the United States in both sides of a civil war, not in the least because America's policy at the time was based on several faulty premises. While the United States was building up China as a great power and continuing ally, the internal position of the Nationalist regime was rapidly eroding; the China to which the United States was committing itself was not to be the China that emerged after the war.

From the beginning, America presumed a gradual democratization of Kuomintang China and tried to pressure Chiang into a series of reforms. But the Nationalist regime was caught in a tragic dead end: the reforms America urged were no doubt necessary to gain popular support, but they undercut the warlords who were among the beleagured government's chief backers.

At the same time, confusion persisted over the nature of the Chinese communists. While there is no truth in subsequent political charges that State Department experts regarded them simply as "agrarian reformers," some believed that the communists would continue their political tactics—the concept of the popular front broadly defined—into the postwar era, while others continued to see no real barrier to a coalition government. In any case, the Nationalists refused to take the communists into the government on terms of equality, dooming to failure the United States inspired effort at coalition as an alternative to civil war.

These confusions marked the postwar missions of Generals Marshall and Wedemeyer. The former sought some middle ground between the communists and the Nationalists, never quite abandoning hope that a coalition was possible. The latter concluded that Chiang's position was probably hopeless but that the United States had no choice but to support him. The policymakers in Washington did not fully accept the first part of the Wedemeyer proposition, nor did they act fully on the second.

The postwar American stance toward Communist China resulted from American domestic political considerations and the developing Cold War in Europe. Before long the prevailing assumption came to be that the Chinese communists regularly winning in the field against Chiang's Nationalist forces were "agents of the Kremlin." An informal, but potent, grouping of businessmen with Asian interests, sincere ideologists, and conservative political leaders emerged as the China Lobby. Congressmen backed by this lobby insisted on increased aid to Chiang as the price for their support of such key postwar policies as the Marshall Plan. Thus, on the eve of communist victory in China, the American commitment to Chiang was being strengthened, even though, short of direct intervention by American forces, it was too late to implement it.

Many American policymakers were, and some still are, convinced that major communist aggression was deterred by the success of the containment policy in Europe. Concluding that containment had worked against the U.S.S.R., the United States applied similar strictures against China. Some saw the "communist take-over" as a single, global design; Dean Rusk, when he was Assistant Secretary of State for Far Eastern Affairs in the nineteen-fifties, contended that the communist victory in China had been Soviet-engineered and that the new regime in Peking was a satellite of Moscow. Chinese entry into the Korean War presumably proved the point.

As the theory of monolithic world communism came into disrepute, militant anti-communists "changed devils in the middle of the stream." For them, China replaced the Soviet Union as the primary threat, and Chinese containment became the cornerstone of American security.

The State Department's China White Paper of August, 1949, was a major document of the postwar period. In his transmittal statement, Secretary Acheson admitted that the policy of support to the Kuomintang had failed, but he seemed also to say that it had been correct. Reasserting the belief that the Chinese communist regime was a creature of the Soviet Union, Mr. Acheson called for a policy that would "encourage all developments in China that now and in the future work toward [helping China] throw off the foreign yoke."

The White Paper was aimed at preparing official and public opinion for the rapidly approaching moment of truth in China. It came at the time Chiang and his regime were fleeing to Formosa. In the United States charges and countercharges of betrayal flew back and forth, and one of the recurring themes of the McCarthy era emerged, the charge that pro-communists had infiltrated the State Department.

Whether the White Paper was also designed to prepare the way for acceptance and recognition of Communist China is not clear. At one time even John Foster Dulles felt that ultimately the United States should recognize the mainland regime. The record is ambiguous, however. Like the Bolsheviks in 1917, the Chinese communists delighted in hurling strong invective at their ideological opponents. Mao, in particular, expressed bitter resentment of American aid to the Nationalist forces, and American diplomats in China were accorded humiliating treatment. The quickly-concluded Chinese alliance with Moscow encouraged the popular American belief that the communist victory in China represented an extension of Soviet power in Asia.

American tradition argued against recognition of the revolutionary regime. Woodrow Wilson's refusal to acknowledge unacceptable revolutionary governments, first in Mexico and then in the Soviet Union, had set the moral tone of modern American foreign policy. The Calvinist tradition was invoked: moral worth and worldly success were intertwined, and, on the holy note that an immoral regime could not succeed, the People's Republic of China was denied recognition.

The United States was apparently not at that time contemplating a binding commitment to the refugee Nationalist regime on Taiwan. In early January, 1950, President Truman announced that the United States would avoid any "involvement in a civil conflict in China" and would provide no "military aid or advice" to Chiang's forces, although it would continue to provide economic aid. This was followed by Secretary Acheson's famous "defensive perimeter" speech, which apparently excluded Taiwan from Asian areas the United States would defend.

In one sense, the Korean War clarified American policy toward China. The outbreak of that conflict precluded any lingering possibility of American recognition. The Seventh Fleet was dispatched to the Taiwan Strait to protect Taiwan. China's entry into the war five months later was branded as unprovoked aggression not only against the United States but against the United Nations, under whose flag the Americans conducted their Korean War effort. Mao became the leading villain in the United States press, and the American policy of containment of communism now meant containment of China.

The ultimate, heavy American involvement in Southeast Asia is obviously a primary offshoot of United States China policy, although this was officially conceded only in 1967 when Secretary Rusk formally cited the threat of Chinese aggression as the principal reason for pursuing the war in Vietnam. The United States has maintained firm opposition to Communist China in the United Nations, variously emphasizing that the Peking regime is illegal, immoral, non-permanent, and, after the Korean conflict, "at war" with the United Nations.

Non-recognition, originally predicated on the assumption that communism in China would be short-lived and was only a Soviet front, is defended in both moral and practical terms. Not even *de facto* recognition without an exchange of diplomats has official favor, although it regularly receives potent endorsement even from such conservatives as Senator Russell of Georgia, who said near the end of 1968: "I have weakened somewhat in my opposition to any dealings at all with the Chinese. I am not willing to bring them into the United Nations just now, but I think it would be a step for the welfare of this country and of the world if we could have some kind of intercourse or exchange with them on some kind of level, even if it was just some kind of a minister to China and they had one here."

Within the past two years some American officials and academicians have proposed ending or moderating the attempt to isolate the People's Republic of China while maintaining the policy of containment. When Professor A. Doak Barnett suggested containment without isolation at the Foreign Relations Committee hearings in 1966, then Vice-President Humphrey, repeating the formula three days later, said it should be a basic part of the United States position toward China.

Others, perhaps most forcefully Professor Morgenthau of

Chicago, insist that such a position is unrealistic. Professor Morgenthau points out that the policy of isolation has failed in that the People's Republic of China does have diplomatic, cultural, and commercial relations with many nations, including major American allies; that no one expects Chiang to return to the mainland; and that such effective isolation as China suffers is either enforced by the communist world or self-inflicted. Since the American policy of isolation is no longer important to China, Professor Morgenthau argues, the United States can expect no favorable response by giving it up. He sees the decisive issue as containment, involving both the commitment to Taiwan and the military alliances on the mainland.

In the eyes of those who agree with Professor Morgenthau, improved American relations with China are impossible under a containment policy, and if it is continued, war may be likely. In this view, Chinese influence in Asia will expand one way or another until it becomes, if not predominant, at least extensive. Morgenthau says, "The United States can no more contain Chinese influence in Asia by arming Thailand and fighting in South Vietnam than China could contain American influence in the Western Hemisphere by arming, say, Nicaragua and fighting in Lower California." Hence, if the United States is determined to prevent China from becoming the dominant power on the Asian mainland, it must strike at China herself; to be effective, this means conquest.

Morgenthau and those who hold similar views believe Chinese predominance does not depend upon military adventures and doubt the likelihood of any Chinese effort to conquer all Asia. If she were to try such a course, they point out, American peripheral containment would be inadequate because China will always enjoy local military superiority. If China has true imperial ambitions, she could be deterred only by the threat of nuclear retaliation. This view denies the validity of the domino theory and insists that Asian revolutions are caused by local conditions rather than by the conscious design of the Chinese or anyone else.

On the other hand, a group of scholars representing what might be called moderate official United States views holds opinions like those of Professor Robert A. Scalopino of Berkeley. They see China as an important factor in communist revolutionary movements spreading across Asia. Even if the Chinese do not actually instigate the actions of Ho Chi Minh's Vietnam communists, such a war of national liberation proves the validity of Mao's basic thesis, and its success in Vietnam would encourage similar ventures elsewhere, enhancing the prestige of Peking and discouraging resistance to communism. Thus, the United States must maintain a military presence in Asia and give military aid to anti-communist regimes, above all, of course, to Taiwan. Adherents to this point of view believe that easing attempts to isolate Peking, while maintaining the policy of containment, will impress on the Chinese communist leaders of the future the necessity for moderating their course and accepting non-communist and even anti-communist states on their borders. Chinese enmity for the United States, they believe, exists for ideological reasons, regardless of the American military presence on the Asian mainland.

Beyond these specific differences of opinion, certain general American postures are significant. All great powers suffer from ethnocentrism, and the United States is no exception. Long isolated from world affairs by the oceans and their own preoccupation with internal development, Americans are not generally knowledgeable when it comes to foreign countries and Asian cultures, especially those in areas outside the historical influence of Western Europe.

Both a result and a cause of America's isolation from the real world of China is the absence of adequate expertise in the State Department. Prior to, during, and immediately after the Second World War, the United States had an exceptionally able group of diplomats who knew China from years of residence as well as from intensive academic study. Even with a normal margin of error in their observations and predictions, the reporting of these career foreign service officers was never as wide of the mark as that, say, of Ambassador Hurley, a Republican appointee of President Roosevelt. Credible evidence that the State Department's China experts were tainted by sympathy for communism, as freely charged in the McCarthy era, has never been forthcoming. Nevertheless, this group was dissipated through dismissal, resignation, or transfer in a wave of anti-communist hysteria. Some departed in disgust; others became political sacrifices served up to appease a public opinion misled into thinking the United States had "lost" China as the result of betrayal, or at least soft-headedness, in the State Department.

In the absence of responsible foreign service officers grounded in Chinese affairs, American China policy from 1950 to the present has been peculiarly susceptible to molding by politicians, diplomats devoid of area expertise, and officials unwilling or unable to stand against the emotional tide of the times. Virtually no Americans have had experience in Communist China, and few, including our academic experts, have any first-hand knowledge of the leaders of a regime that has held power for twenty years.

Perhaps an even more important factor than the lack of diplomatic expertise has been what General de Gaulle calls *immobilisme*. In order to gain support for a policy, decision-makers feel it necessary to stimulate public opinion to a high emotional pitch. All too often they become prisoners of their own handiwork, unable to change direction even when they see its desirability, for fear of losing public support. As an illustration, in the 1952 election campaign the Republicans accused the Democrats of having "lost" China because they were "soft on communism." But in 1954, when President Eisenhower declined to intervene militarily in Indochina the Democrats accused the Republicans of "appeasement."

The current impasse in United States-China relations stems in part from a genuine American inability to understand how Peking can conceive of United States policy as aggressive. Beyond the Taiwan question, the United States rejects the idea that China could logically suspect the aggressive intent of American military operations that occur on China's very borders. Such a view prevailed at the time of the Chinese intervention in the Korean conflict and still holds sway today. Former Secretary Rusk, for example, asserted recently that the Communist Chinese "knew" American bombings near the Chinese border, a part of the Vietnam war operation, did not really threaten China herself.

The basic question for American foreign policy is whether stability on the Asian mainland can be achieved while the

United States maintains an Asian military presence regarded by China as hostile. The issue here is not the propriety of American influence in Asia; it is the effect of military methods and military alliances in promoting, or eroding, the American influence. Few serious critics of United States policy advocate a sudden American withdrawal from all of Asia, given the intricacies of the American involvement, but many believe the United States should seek to reduce and to defuse its military commitments on the mainland. The presence of an American fleet in the far Pacific, if the Taiwan problem were solved, would not necessarily be a serious factor in relations with China, but troops and permanent bases on the mainland are clearly another matter. Related is the broader question of how the United States views the contemporary world and its role in it. The policies and attitudes of the People's Republic of China will, of course, play an important part in the answers to these questions, but the United States, if it so desires, has a wide area for initiative.

The question is open and the hour is late.

THE CONGRESS AND AMERICAN ASIAN POLICY

JOHN SHERMAN COOPER:

While the Executive Branch has jurisdiction to take initiatives in foreign policy, the influence of the Congress and the people it represents, either to resist or to support change, could be a determining factor in our future course. This influence, as we know so well, has been demonstrated with respect to Vietnam. As a member of the United States Senate, perhaps I can clarify Congressional attitudes on present China policy, exploring in particular the possibility of the Congress supporting a modification.

Great bitterness remains in the Congress and in the country over the communist take-over of China. This bitterness derives in part from a widely held opinion, sentimental and exaggerated, that the prewar American relationship with China was special as a result of our long-standing trade and the selfless service of our missionaries. Our attachment to China was strengthened, also, by our admiration for the Nationalist Chinese who, under critical conditions, refused to surrender during their long struggle against the Japanese.

America reacted strongly to the reality of communist expansion in Eastern Europe after World War II and the threat of extended communist influence over the vast continent of Asia. Our experience in the Korean War did not lessen American anxiety. And whatever the merits of the issues involving Communist China, India, and Tibet, China's actions toward these countries, and its training and support of anti-government forces in Laos, Thailand, and South Vietnam, have lent credibility to the view that Communist China is set on an aggressive and expansionist course.

This view of Communist China has been expressed clearly

in a series of treaties and resolutions approved overwhelmingly by the Congress. The United States has entered into security treaties with Australia and New Zealand, the Philippines, the Republic of Korea, the Republic of China, Japan, and the SEATO countries, including the protocol states of South Vietnam, Cambodia, and Laos. Each of these treaties commits the United States in case of "an armed attack" on a specified geographical area to "act to meet the common danger in accordance with its Constitutional processes," although "Constitutional process" is nowhere defined. The Formosa Resolution of 1955 granted to the President broad powers to employ the armed forces to defend Formosa, the Pescadores, Quemoy, and Matsu; and the Tonkin Gulf Resolution of 1964 gave the President much broader authority to take all necessary steps not only to repel an armed attack but also to "prevent further aggression."

Year after year the Congress expresses its view upon another aspect of containment—China's participation in world trade—by amendments offered to many bills barring United States trade with third countries that have commercial relations with North Vietnam and China. And last year the Administration recommended and the Congress authorized and appropriated funds for the deployment of a so-called thin ABM system for protection against the nuclear-weapons capability of Communist China. Many in the Executive Branch and in the Congress feel that, regardless of whether she proceeds with considered purpose or irrational fervor, Communist China's development of nuclear weapons is a threat to the countries of Asia and to the United States. Communist China's public statements, her propaganda, and her behavior toward the United States support the dominant belief that she is implacably hostile and that she would not respond to our initiatives for a better relationship.

Nevertheless, the judgment of many scholars and those who know China and Asia better than the vast majority of our people is that the United States should seek an improved relationship, amounting even to a major modification of present policy. Their recommendations and the hearings held by the Senate Foreign Relations Committee in 1966 have made an impact upon the Congress.

Our experience in the Vietnam War, perhaps more than anything else, has brought into question and debate the policy of containment. We have learned that our country, possessing the greatest military power in the world, could not and did not wish to use its full power. From a moral standpoint, the United States could not destroy the countries of North and South Vietnam. As a responsible nation, it had to consider the ramifications of Chinese and Soviet intervention and a military engagement that could lead to nuclear war. We have also learned that the appeal and strength of nationalism can be directed against the United States by friend or foe, however good our motives may be.

Scholars stress that China's foreign policy has been basically defensive; that her invasion of India was to assert a legitimate boundary claim and to discredit a rival Asian power; that Tibet is traditionally a part of greater China; that Chinese assistance to North Vietnam is primarily a protest against the United States presence; and that Chinese activities in neighboring countries are in reaction to the threat of encirclement by America and other hostile nations, including the U.S.S.R. Perhaps these claims accurately represent the Chinese point of view, but Chinese policy, in its militant expression, often offends and clashes with the legitimate interests of other nations. The stringency of China's demands and her inflexible hostility make it difficult for the Executive to recommend, and the Congress to support, changes in American policy.

On the other hand, China's desire to preserve and strengthen her national identity and to take her place among the great powers is natural. A nation of China's geographical position, size, population, and long history has a rightful claim to a position of influence among the nations of Asia. The United States must recognize that Communist China fears a bipolar world dominated by the United States and the Soviet Union and, with this in mind, consider what changes in policy America can appropriately make.

The United States has important security interests, economic ties, and diplomatic relations in Asia that need to be maintained. Lately, Asian leaders like President Marcos and Foreign Minister Romulo of the Philippines and Lee Kuan

Yew of Singapore have begun to suggest that betterment of their own and American relationships with Communist China is in the long-term interest of all concerned. The need for reëxamination of our Asian policy is recognized, moreover, by an increasing number in the Congress, among them some of its most influential members. The majority leader, Senator Mike Mansfield, long a student of Asian affairs, expressed last year the growing sense that America must reconsider its China policy:

> I urge you to think for yourselves about China. I urge you to approach, with a new objectivity, that vast nation, with its great population of industrious and intelligent people. Bear in mind that the peace of Asia and the world will depend on China as much as it does on this nation, the Soviet Union, or any other, not because China is communist but because China is China—among the largest countries in the world and the most populous.

Other influential men in the Congress are recognizing the necessity of bringing before the Congress and the people the full nature of the issues that face us concerning China.

President Nixon said during his campaign: "The dialogue with Communist China must come, I think, during the two terms of the next President." Much more education and discussion about China must precede any change of attitude on the part of the people of the United States and their elected representatives. The Congress can do much to educate itself and its constituents, supplementing the work of the individual scholars with public hearings and frequent reports. These efforts, however, will be only a beginning, a preliminary to the dialogue suggested by President Nixon. Meanwhile, the cautious and tentative, almost imperceptible, efforts that have been made toward a better relationship must be continued.

THE POWER OF AN AMERICAN PRESIDENT

DON EDWARDS:

Like all American Presidents, Richard Nixon will have freedom of choice in foreign policy, a privilege he will not enjoy in domestic matters. The domestic legislation he proposes must travel the entire Congressional obstacle course and survive if it can the hazards of random seniority power, the buffets of committees and subcommittees, the muscle of the lobbies, the withering effects of the filibuster, and countless other assaults characteristic of the Congressional process. Except for military and space appropriations, the severely disciplined end product, good or bad, seldom approximates the legislation a President proposes; but Mr. Nixon is able to say that the Congress, not he, is primarily responsible if any unfortunate consequences result.

The disciplines of Congressional scrutiny do not apply in foreign affairs. Like Presidents Truman, Eisenhower, Kennedy, and Johnson, Mr. Nixon is free to choose his own policies on foreign trade, on matters of diplomacy and recognition, and on the deployment of American military and intelligence forces. The voices of criticism and dissent in both the Senate and the House are those of a minority, and successive Presidents have discovered that these voices can be ignored unless, as has been the case in Vietnam, the Presidential policies are especially vulnerable.

This omnipotence, while delightful, is a President's greatest peril. Decisions once made are difficult to change and can have undreamed-of consequences, devastating for the United States and the other nations involved. They can shatter the career of the President and emasculate the political party he heads.

While Mr. Nixon has the same latitude in dealing with mainland China that he will be allowed in all foreign affairs, the indications are that he will almost certainly choose a course similar to the one charted by his predecessors: the military containment of China instituted by President Truman in June, 1950, and defined and hardened into the Eisenhower-Dulles policy of isolation, with its attendant prohibitions against recognition, trade, travel, and cultural exchange.

That the United States under President Nixon is virtually certain to reach a negotiated settlement of the Vietnam War should not be interpreted as "new policy" for Asia. The Vietnam War was tolerable as long as it was relatively painless and China's involvement was minimal. It was not until its cost became felt in American homes, in the business and industrial communities, and in the pocketbooks of the general public, that a settlement became politically imperative.

If change is needed in the United States twin policies of containment and isolation of China, neither the people of the country nor most of their elected representatives in Congress indicate awareness of it. Our China policy produces no urban riots, does not accelerate the rise in crime, inflames few students. Except for their reservations about the magnitude of our Vietnam involvement, the vast majority of Americans accept our present role in Asia. It can be presumed that they will support the President in the perpetuation of this role, especially since he can offer proof of nearly unanimous support from the governments of non-communist Asian countries. The State Department can document in papers and speeches that our policy receives the approval not only of client nations like South Korea, the Philippines, Thailand, Taiwan, and South Vietnam but also of the nearly three-quarters of a billion people in Japan, India, Malaysia, Singapore, and Indonesia.

Recommending reconsideration of our China policy is still a rather daring political action in the United States. Influential industrialists and politicians in America do not work constantly for closer commercial and social connections with China as their counterparts do in Japan. In most Congressional districts the candidate who indicates that he favors trade with and travel in China will be subjected to sharp attacks on his patriotism and judgment by his political opponents and by the local press. A majority in the Republican Party and the southern minority in the Democratic Party label any movement toward better relations with China as "soft on communism."

In December, 1968, I sent a questionnaire, to be answered anonymously, to all members of the House of Representatives. Most congressmen throughout the country reported that they might risk political annihilation if they should on their own motion publicly advocate a more open relationship with China at this time. Seventy-six per cent of those responding to the questionnaire expected negative reactions from their constituents to any initiative on their part. The replies went like this:

"They would want me to have a mental examination."
"Political suicide! !"
"Catastrophe."
"Defeat me in the next election!"
"Attempted assassination!"
"Disaster!"
"They would get a new Congressman."
"At the moment I would be defeated!"

Significantly, however, far fewer members of Congress expressed alarm at possible Presidential initiatives on China policy. Of the ninety answers received, only thirty-five per cent indicated that they would be openly critical of such a decision by the President. I doubt that President Nixon would trigger a serious political storm should he decide to soften American policy and offer China trade, travel, and even diplomatic recognition.*

During the 1968 campaign, President Nixon did not discuss China in any detail. Perhaps the best indication of his views can be gleaned from an article appearing in the October, 1967, issue of *Foreign Affairs*. He stated his opposition to "rushing to grant recognition to Peking, to admit it to the United Nations, and to ply it with offers of trade—all of which would serve to confirm its rulers in their present course."

---

*A tabulation of the answers to this questionnaire and additional Congressional comments appear in Appendix III.

He advocated distinguishing "carefully between long-range and short-range policies and fashioning short-range programs so as to advance our long-range goals." But he also declared: "The world cannot be safe until China changes. Thus our aim, to the extent that we can influence events, should be to induce change. The way to do this is to persuade China that she must change, that she cannot satisfy her imperialist ambitions, and that her own national interest requires a turning away from foreign adventuring and a turning inward toward the solution of her own domestic problems."

From these statements and on the basis of his Cabinet choices and his prior political record, I would expect Mr. Nixon to institute little change in American China policy. American political leaders of both parties, American political scientists, and the general public overwhelmingly hold to the conviction—an opinion shared by a vast majority of friendly Asians and Europeans—that Asia, with its surrounding islands and seas, is currently so unstable and is of such strategic importance that the United States must maintain its Asian military bases and its fleet in Asian waters. The United States is not in Asia because of Vietnam or to protect Taiwan from China. It is there because, in appraising the chances for stability in Asia, it concludes that its existing military bases are the defensive perimeter for the United States in the Pacific and because it believes its containment-of-China policy, if not its isolation-of-China policy, is clearly supported by the great non-communist nations of Asia.

The situation becomes more perilous as China perfects her nuclear arsenal and as pressures build up in Asia for an end to America's role of policeman. The Americans will leave, however, only when the non-communist Asian nations insist that they leave. Until peaceful coexistence in Asia is a fact and the non-communist nations can feel secure without the American presence, such a demand is unlikely.

"Japan's dilemma—building a new politics at home and finding a new national role, consistent with deep traditions and industrial strength and the newly discovered political ideals of the West—is a microcosm of the dilemma of all non-Western countries."
George W. Ball

5 # Japan's Changing Focus

A STATEMENT BY
Edwin O. Reischauer

COMMENTS BY:

Tokuma Utsunomiya
Arthur Goldberg
Chester A. Ronning
Shuji Kurauchi

EDWIN O. REISCHAUER:

Relations among the three largest nations that front on the Pacific are closely intertwined today, as indeed they have been for at least half a century. Japan feels herself caught between her two huge Pacific neighbors, the one much larger than Japan in population, the other much greater in productive power. While the relationship with China is a matter of great importance to both Japan and the United States, in each case this relationship is affected by their relations with each other.

China has looked very different during the past two decades as viewed from Japan and from America. The United States, as the major victor in the Pacific war, has been inevitably and deeply involved in the turbulent aftermath of that war— the great revolutionary changes in China, the development of a separate political entity in Taiwan, the Korean War, and the multiple instabilities in Southeast Asia, including the protracted civil strife in Vietnam, unwisely allowed to escalate into a major international war. This bitter history, I feel, has led Americans to concentrate too much on the military approach to peace and stability in East Asia and to make the containment of Chinese aggression too central a theme in their policies.

The Japanese, as the losers in the Pacific war, have found that, whatever the rights or wrongs in each specific case, the violent aftermath of World War II could be left to others to handle while they concentrated on the restoration of their own society and the reconstruction of fruitful relations with their neighbors. In particular, they have been much concerned with restoring full and friendly relations with China because this largest of all countries is not only geographically close to Japan but is, in a sense, her cultural motherland; and before the war China was of major economic importance to Japan.

The Japanese, influenced by their racial and cultural affinity for the Chinese, approach the China problem with a different emotional emphasis than the Americans. China is to Japan, after all, what the Mediterranean world and Greece and Rome are to the United States. Japan feels a much greater need, therefore, to repair her relationship with the Chinese than does America across the vast Pacific.

Japan also nurtures a feeling that her trade with China is of great importance to her. Part of this feeling, I think, is a delusion. For a hundred years the outside world has been deluded about what four hundred million Chinese customers—or, as they are now, nearly eight hundred million Chinese customers—might buy. They have never bought it, and I do not think they will buy it in the future. The Chinese economy is much weaker and smaller than Japan's. I think present Japanese trade with China has expanded as far as the Chinese economy can allow; it accounts for only about three percent of Japan's total trade, although it amounts to fifteen per cent of Chinese foreign trade.

The American and Japanese approaches to the Chinese problem have differed sharply, but each has been possible only because of the relationship of Japan and the United States to each other. Without bases in Japan and the support of Japanese economic power and technical skills, the United States could not have done what it has in East Asia during the past two decades. Conversely, without American military protection, Japan could not have withdrawn so completely from the conflicts and tensions of that part of the world and concentrated so fully on her own narrow interests.

This picture is now changing radically. On the one hand, the United States has learned through the bitter experience of Vietnam the limitations of the military approach and the more basic lesson that the rising spirit of nationalism throughout Asia is a most effective defense against outside domination. On the other hand, Japan has become the third largest economic power in the world and can no longer abstract herself from the problems of East Asia. From now on she must play a leading role in their solution. Thus, the once-differing perspectives on China from Japan and from the United States are rapidly merging into a single focus.

Some Japanese may believe that Japan can continue to avoid involvement in the problems of East Asia. More specifically, some think that by eliminating or at least reducing the defense relationship with the United States, Japan can achieve a position of greater neutrality from which a rapprochement with China might prove easier to accomplish. Underlying this concept is usually the assumption that the United States would continue to maintain something of its present military posture in the western Pacific regardless of its relationship with Japan. This, I believe, is a fundamental conceptual error.

Without Japanese bases and, more important, Japanese coöperation, the United States would probably find it too costly, difficult, and hazardous to maintain its defense commitment to South Korea, for example, or its present deployment of the Seventh Fleet. But the security of South Korea is probably of greater concern to Japan than to the United States, and the safety of the sea approaches to Japan, which the Seventh Fleet maintains, is vital to the Japanese economy. If denied Japanese bases and support, the United States would probably find it expedient to withdraw its military power to mid-Pacific. In that case, Japan, at a minimum, would be forced to create a substitute for the Seventh Fleet to secure her maritime lifelines and would probably find herself deeply involved in other ways in the security problems of that part of the world. In turn, a rearmed Japan would stir up new fears among the nations she once despoiled and might also find herself in a hostile military confrontation with China that would prove even less favorable for rapprochement than her present stance.

On the other hand, if we assume the continuation of the Japanese-American defense relationship, which is certainly more to Japan's interest than rearmament would be, Japan in the future will probably have to undertake greater responsibility for the nature and form of this relationship than in the past. Since the military posture of the United States in the western Pacific depends heavily on its security treaty with Japan and is maintained in large part for Japan's benefit, this posture should, and I believe will, in time be determined as much by Japan as by the United States.

Such reasoning may sound discouraging to those who believe that Japan's close association with the United States prevents the development of a satisfactory relationship with China. But this, I believe, is not a correct assumption for the future, and I do not think that it applies very well even to the recent past. In the fifties there was some basis for this line of reasoning, but since then it has lost most of its validity. Non-recognition of Peking is not a price Japan pays for trade with America or defense by it. Others of our closest allies, the United Kingdom and Canada, to name but two, have taken very different approaches to the Chinese problem without strain on their relations with the United States.

Factors other than her American relations explain the failure of Japan to achieve a satisfactory understanding with Peking. One has been Japanese economic and political involvement with Taiwan and other strongly anti-Peking countries, such as South Korea and the Philippines. Japan's trade with Taiwan alone is four-fifths as great as its trade with continental China. A sharp readjustment of relations with Peking would seriously strain Japan's economic and political ties with a number of her close and important neighbors. Actually, relations with these countries are even more inhibiting to Japan's China policy than to America's.

A second factor is the attitude of China. In recent years she has not had happy relations with any important foreign country. Those industrialized nations that have extended her recognition, such as the United Kingdom and France, have not been able to establish as meaningful contact as has Japan through her limited formula of "the separation of economics and politics." On the other hand, Japan's effort to appear neutral has, I believe, impeded rather than helped rapprochement with Peking. This pose has encouraged the Chinese in their unrealistic hope that Japan can be detached from her close and absolutely essential relationship with the other major industrialized nations and drawn instead into a position of subservience to China. Such fantasies simply delay the day when China will accept a more realistic and mutually beneficial relationship with the outside world. In my view, a Japan that stood a little more firmly on her own interests and beliefs would have more chance of achieving a rapprochement with China than a Japan that feigns a neutrality she cannot in fact maintain.

Still, it must be admitted that the tensions between the United States and China do cast a shadow over Japanese-Chinese relations, particularly since it is commonly assumed in both Japan and China that Japanese foreign policy is set by the United States. I believe that American control of Japanese foreign policy exists only in the minds of those who assume it; it is a feeling rather than a fact. For several years the United States has made no specific effort to direct Japan's China policy. Japan is by now in a position to develop her own policy if the Japanese can realize that they are free of American restraints. Japan's China policy probably would resemble present American foreign policy in many respects since the basic interests of the two countries are so similar.

Japan has more capacity than the United States to lead in the direction of bringing China into the community of nations. Already Japan has cultural and trade relations with China; Japan is the greatest trading partner China has. Even with the real restraints like the Taiwan problem that make reconciliation difficult, Japan has the latitude to go beyond cultural and commercial exchange. The Japanese public overwhelmingly favors improved relations with Communist China, and I suspect that formulas can be found to implement this national will even while the Taiwan issue remains unresolved.

With regard to Taiwan, neither the Japanese nor the American public would find it morally justified or practically wise to try to force the inhabitants of Taiwan into the arms of Peking against their will. This would run counter to the belief in self-determination both peoples share and shake the confidence of other nations in their reliability and sense of justice. While it might be convenient for the United States and Japan in their relations with China if Taiwan were to disappear as a separate entity, Taiwan does in fact exist and is probably going to go on complicating their relations with China. To pretend otherwise is to start on a false basis in seeking a rapprochement with China.

In disentangling itself from the Vietnam War, the United States is likely to pull back militarily to some extent and possibly out of the whole of continental Southeast Asia. If American and Japanese attempts at rapprochement with China are handled in a clumsy manner, an increased sense of insecurity in Southeast Asia could result. If approached skillfully, a policy of rapprochement and military pullback, by lessening tensions between China and the United States, could strengthen rather than weaken the security of China's neighbors.

Hitherto divergent American and Japanese perspectives on China should and will, as these present trends indicate, merge into a single focus. But there will remain one clear difference between the two countries in their China policy. Japan has much more to fear from tensions and turmoil in East Asia than does the United States and much more to gain from the relaxation of these tensions and the development of peace, stability, and prosperity. Japan has all the more reason, therefore, to take the lead in moving toward a rapprochement with China. The Chinese are in most ways far more responsive to Japanese than to Americans. The most likely way for China to find her way back to a mutually satisfactory relationship with the outside world may be through the development of better relations with Japan. For this reason, Japan should not be adapting herself grudgingly to what she considers a too restrictive American policy toward China. Instead, Japan herself should be developing a more forward-looking policy to which the United States could later happily adjust its stance.

We would be foolish to assume that the Chinese will respond quickly to Japanese and American efforts at rapprochement. Conditions are too chaotic in China today and the hostilities against the outside world too deeply rooted to make any favorable response likely in the near future. But a gradual relaxation of tensions and ultimately the acceptance of peaceful coexistence and mutual coöperation would certainly be more likely if Japan were to take the lead in thawing the present frozen position.

TOKUMA UTSUNOMIYA:

I agree with Professor Reischauer that Japan can and should go ahead independently to achieve a better relationship with China. But in Japan we have a paradox. The people of Japan and the people of the United States view China quite differently. Americans regard the distant mainland of China as such a threat that they feel their nuclear base on Okinawa is essential to their security. The Japanese, living much closer to China, should be even more apprehensive, but the majority give little thought to China as a menace. The Japanese government bases its China policy on American fears of Peking, not on the much less intense Japanese attitude. Here we have the paradox and in it the barrier to an independent Japanese foreign policy.

CHESTER A. RONNING:

More than once Canadian policy regarding China has been determined by the United States attitude. As John King Fairbank has pointed out, American attitudes, even at the highest levels, are based largely on emotion. I am sure that the United States has no deliberate policy of controlling the foreign relationships of either Japan or Canada, but whenever Canada has felt the pressure of American emotional resistance, she has pulled in her horns, particularly if it has seemed that going contrary to the United States position might be injurious to the United Nations. As a result, the Canadian government gives perpetual consideration to a more positive China policy but, so far, has never come to a firm decision.* I cannot help but feel that Japan and Canada are in the same boat. If influential Canadians and Japanese on opposite sides of the Pacific who wish to see a change of policy persist in their efforts, perhaps together they can influence their governments to make independent decisions on China.

ARTHUR GOLDBERG:

Does the United States exert pressure on Canada and Japan to prevent a relaxation of their China policies? In my experience, we have not welcomed Canada's moves toward a more flexible China policy. With respect to Japan, we have exhibited less concern because, so far, the Japanese government has seemed less ready to make radical moves. In the past two years, when the Italians have proposed a commission to study the whole question of Communist China's admission to the United Nations, the Japanese delegation has shown the greatest reluctance to give its support; it did so only after insisting on guarantees that the study commission would in no way threaten the Important Question Resolution.**

Initial United States support of the Italian proposal was largely tactical, in response to a broader Canadian initiative that we did not believe timely or well-advised, and on that basis we appealed to Japan to support the Italian proposal also. Perhaps our more recent support of the Italian resolu-

---

*The Secretary of State for External Affairs, Mr. Mitchell Sharp, announced in the House of Commons on February 10, 1969, that the Canadian Embassy in Stockholm had been instructed to get in touch with the Embassy of the People's Republic of China to propose that talks concerning relations between the two countries be held at "a mutually convenient time and place in the near future."

**This resolution, adopted in 1961, requires a two-thirds majority of the General Assembly to effect any change in the representation of China in the United Nations.

tion, in the face of firm opposition from Taiwan, can be regarded as an opening wedge in the effort to bring mainland China into membership. I think, objectively, we can consider it a beginning, since the Canadian attitude did not affect our later support for the Italian proposal.

SHUJI KURAUCHI:

While I feel quite certain, along with Ambassador Reischauer, that United States influence is not a determining factor in shaping Japanese policy, not all Japanese take such a tolerant view. Many believe that Japan's rapid postwar recovery was made possible only by Japanese subservience to United States policy in the Far East. This viewpoint is not limited to certain sectors of the Japanese people; it has frequently been expressed in Korea and has gained credence throughout Southeast Asia.

President Chung Hee Park of South Korea has implied that Japan's swift return to prosperity was achieved through the sacrifice of his own country during the Korean War. He uses this line of reasoning as a propaganda technique, attributing Japan's current well-being to United States aid and the profits being reaped by the Japanese munitions industry from America's involvement in the Vietnam War. President Park extends his doctrinaire argument to suggest that the United States is grooming Japan for a military role in Asia similar to the one it expects West Germany to play in Europe.

From these propagandistic statements arises the specter of Japanese rearmament. Many Japanese fear that as the United States moves to make Japan its successor as the policeman of the Pacific, rearmament will naturally follow. Moreover, as Japan's trade and investments expand in Southeast Asia, Japanese in increasing numbers will be entering areas they once occupied militarily. Doubt about Japanese motives is bound to increase, and with it the adverse propaganda.

"Those who see communist ideology as an all-conquering virus may prefer to discount history and omit it from their diagnosis. But to understand China without history, to divorce this most historical-minded of all cultures from its past, is quite impossible."
John King Fairbank

6

The Aggressive People's Republic of China: Menace or Myth?

A COLLOQUY AMONG:

Edwin O. Reischauer
J.W. Fulbright
Mark O. Hatfield
Masumi Ezaki

AMBASSADOR REISCHAUER: In the United States the chief emphasis has been on the menace of China. It is strange that we Americans, far across the Pacific and a much stronger nation, should fear China in a way that the Japanese do not. Frankly, I would side with the Japanese. I think they view China much more realistically than we.

SENATOR FULBRIGHT: We have based our policy and our feelings on certain assumptions. We assumed, of course, that all communist regimes were joined together indissolubly in a conspiratorial compact to conquer the world. And we have treated the communist countries as a monolithic entity of awesome power and frightening potential. It is not too surprising, then, that we have regarded China as a hostile and aggressive nation that is threatening to impose communism on Asia by force just as the Soviet Union imposed its ideology on central Europe.

AMBASSADOR REISCHAUER: The real question we in America must face is not whether China as a communist power would like to see other people have revolutions. We must look at the record and decide if China is an expansionist, aggressive, militarily dangerous country. My own answer would be that she is not a great danger.

SENATOR FULBRIGHT: I do not see that the present Chinese government has made any serious attempt to expand its territory beyond its present borders. The Chinese forces that fought us in Korea are no longer there. North Korea has, in fact, become less pro-Chinese and more neutral in the

Sino-Soviet dispute in recent years. Nor did Chinese forces remain in India. And in the case of Tibet, the Chinese took over a territory that both Peking and the Nationalist government have long regarded as Chinese.

AMBASSADOR REISCHAUER: We do have to face the reality that the Chinese have gone across their borders on three occasions, but we should look at each case from their point of view, not just from our own. I think they honestly thought of their entry into the Korean War as self-defense, remembering that this was the route by which Japan had extended its empire into China. They thought *we* were coming to attack *them* in North Korea. Against the Indians their military action amounted to a small correction of the border, and I don't think they had any intention of seizing and trying to hold parts of India. Today they do have a certain number of labor troops, but not combatants, in Vietnam. Again they probably view their presence there more in terms of self-defense than of conquest.

SENATOR FULBRIGHT: In the past few years we have begun to talk about China and to think about China in somewhat different terms. The assumption of a monolithic communist world is obviously no longer valid. The widely different paths followed in the European communist world by the Soviet Union, Yugoslavia, Rumania, and Albania are by now generally well-recognized, although the diversities among communist states and parties in Asia are less familiar. As one commentator has put it, communism is "a many-splintered thing." Yet our policy has remained unchanged even though the events of the last two decades should have caused us to question our original assumptions.

AMBASSADOR REISCHAUER: We should be careful to stick to the facts when we try to reassess. Some people make the case that China has always been a pacifistic nation and has not wanted to expand. This is nonsense. All great empires have tended to expand as far as they could or as far as they felt they needed to. The Chinese expanded northward and westward to subdue the mobile, nomadic peoples who were menacing China Proper. As a result China became a great empire. China is today, and has been, one of the great imperialist countries, ruling thousands of square miles inhabited by millions of non-Chinese—Mongols, Turks, Tibetans, and so forth.

China has never pushed in the other directions, however, to the south or to the east. She did in earlier times occasionally invade Korea; she has invaded North Vietnam, but not recently; and once or twice in history she has entered Burma. Until the recent border clash only once before have Chinese and Indians fought each other, a long time ago, somewhere around 842 A.D. The Chinese never felt themselves menaced from the south or the east and therefore have had no strong traditions of expansion in those directions. Their attitude toward Vietnam or Burma or Thailand is very different from their feeling about Tibet.

SENATOR HATFIELD: I would think that the greatest threat to China's neighbors is not the unlikely possibility of invasion by Chinese Communist forces but the threat of internal subversion encouraged by Peking.

SENATOR FULBRIGHT: China has certainly encouraged and supported insurrections and wars of national liberation but, as far as I am aware, has not participated directly. There have been threats of direct participation, but China has not suited her actions to her words.

Certainly, the Peking government hopes that wars of national liberation will succeed not only in Vietnam but in Laos, Thailand, Burma, and other Asian countries. They have made no secret of their desire in this regard. But a desire to see such wars succeed, a desire that is no stronger than our desire to see them fail, is one thing. Ability to insure success is quite another.

AMBASSADOR REISCHAUER: If we look at what the Chinese say about their present policies and what they do about them, I think we must be impressed that they talk about revolution throughout the world and not about conquest or aggression.

They are happy to help other people have revolutions. They are glad to supply do-it-yourself kits to others. They don't talk much about going elsewhere and doing it for them, nor have they tried.

SENATOR HATFIELD: Many experts have made the point that wars of national liberation can be successful only in a climate of political instability where the economic, social, and political grievances of the people are ignored or suppressed. Unless we send in enough men to constitute an occupation force, as we have in Vietnam, the American military cannot be expected to maintain stability in the face of these conditions. On the contrary, I believe it is demonstrable that our military presence heightens instability by stimulating the nationalistic sensitivies of the people.

American foreign policymakers could learn a lesson from the nursery rhyme: "All the king's horses and all the king's men couldn't put Humpty Dumpty together again." With all our military resources and all of our men, we cannot reconstruct a stability that has been shattered by political revolution. Like our Japanese colleagues, I think our most effective course would be to prevent the nations of Southeast Asia from falling into chaos by providing economic and technical assistance. If, in spite of our efforts, progress is too slow or political and social justice too remote, we must expect that communist-led revolutions may succeed.

SENATOR FULBRIGHT: I suspect that the fears some Asians express about direct Chinese expansion or indirect Chinese intervention are often rationalizations, attempts to blame internal infirmities on external factors. Wars of national liberation can be and are supported from the outside. So are attempts to defeat them. But it seems to me that they are essentially home-grown products that sprout from complaints and frustrations, nourished by government ineffectiveness, lack of interest, and corruption.

I doubt that China presently could be successful as an expansionist military power even if she desired to be one. The Chinese have a powerful land army capable of defending the mainland against almost any combination of forces, but if mobile forces, strategically positioned, are necessary for expansion, it is we and not the Chinese who have that potential. If the evidence of a capacity and a desire to expand is the presence of a country's troops outside its own territory, what conclusion can we draw when the only Chinese soldiers outside China are engineer and air defense units in North Vietnam while, in Asia alone, we have more than half a million troops in South Vietnam, over fifty thousand in South Korea, and some forty thousand in Thailand? What about our naval and air installations in Japan, the Philippines, Taiwan, Okinawa, Guam, and elsewhere?

AMBASSADOR REISCHAUER: The Chinese are a fundamentally inward-looking civilization, and well they might be. They are by all odds the largest unit of people in the world. One of the great miracles of human history is that this huge mass of people has held together as a single, successful political unit for the better part of two thousand years. Since they are part of such a large unit, the Chinese have always tended to look in at themselves rather than out at the fringe of barbarians beyond China. They have regarded all foreigners either as closer, semi-civilized barbarians like the other East Asians or as more distant, hopelessly barbaric peoples like those in Europe.

Today China has great problems that make her all the more inward-looking, and it seems improbable that she will turn outward for quite some time. China suffers from gigantism. Being a nation of seven to eight hundred million people has great disadvantages, and the problems connected with her huge size and her low economic base will keep China absorbed in herself for the foreseeable future.

The Chinese are also susceptible to a phenomenon I call culturalism. It's a little different from nationalism, closer perhaps to the popular modern term, racism. They are egocentric and have great difficulty extending their influence to other parts of the world. Their efforts in Africa illustrate this problem of culturalism. Africans very soon found out that the Chinese are every bit as arrogant as the whites. They are not interested in the black people as such and are unwilling as yet to accept them as equals. Culturalism will make even their more subtle efforts to help worldwide revolution somewhat unlikely to succeed.

When we consider all these realities, present as well as past, I think we have greatly overestimated the threat of China and have been wrong to base so much of our effort on the concept of containment.

MR. EZAKI: Two years ago I visited Peking. I am a pro-American politician, and I was not sure the Chinese would welcome me. I went there to find out whether there was any possibility of war breaking out between the United States and China. Perhaps because I was a director of the Japanese National Self-Defense Agency, the Peking government decided to show me the People's Liberation Army. I do not know, but they may have been trying to send a message to the United States through me. In any case, what I saw primarily were land forces equipped with obsolete arms. Their tanks, for example, were vintage 1958.

They gave me a demonstration of guerrilla warfare. There was a shack. One of the trainees opened the door and went in. There was an explosion. Then the trainee, acting hungry, opened a pot on the stove. Another explosion. He grabbed a cigarette. Another explosion. Obviously the Chinese were trying to tell me that they would resort to guerrilla warfare if their country should be invaded.

All the methods and equipment I saw were primitive in the extreme. Their army could never face the tremendous military power of the United States in conventional warfare.

What struck me, however, was that here were close to eight hundred million people being driven by their leaders in a single direction. Their resentment against both the Soviet Union and the United States was being fanned at every opportunity. All the Chinese women I saw were dressed in one color, brownish black. They wore no lipstick. Obviously they were thinking in terms of preparing for war.

In China isolation produces vast ignorance of the outside world. My guide was a student at Peking University, one of the two largest universities in China. This young intellectual told me: "You people are still under American occupation. We understand that you are still living in poverty and are starving." To have an intellectual attending one of the great universities say that to me was appalling. Complete isolation and ignorance are fearful things. And these are the people being contained and prevented from having outside contact by the United States.

SENATOR HATFIELD: I believe Peking's belligerency and militancy are not just the products of China's century of humiliation. I think they are also frustrated reactions to our refusal to treat them as equals. One of the troubles with Americans is our propensity to think we are superior in every way. It's perfectly all right, for instance, for the United States to have "the bomb" because we are a peace-loving nation, but it's not all right for the Chinese to have it because they are barbarians with no concern for human life. We think it's reasonable for the United States, under the Monroe Doctrine, to keep possibly hostile foreign nations away from our borders and out of our hemisphere. But when the Chinese rather impotently rant and rave and issue aggressive declarations about *our* military bases on *their* borders, we solemnly nod our heads and interpret their rhetoric as a determination to dominate Asia and, if possible, the world.

Just as we take a rather smug view of our moral superiority, we think that our institutions and political system must be inherently superior. Because they have worked remarkably well for us, we assume that they will inevitably be accepted by others. Certainly, some socialist systems have adapted capitalist principles and incentives to fit their own needs, but that doesn't mean all communist countries in the future will, or should.

Another thing we do is interpret Chinese rhetoric and actions in the worst possible light in order to confirm our own negative view of them. People tend to perform as others expect them to, and we risk creating self-fulfilling prophesies when we talk darkly of China's "nuclear blackmail" of her neighbors or sourly and loudly predict that she would be irresponsibly disruptive if she were admitted to the United Nations. No one expects American policymakers to sit around thinking only good thoughts about the Chinese, but we do not need to give a perverse sanction to their hostile and belligerent actions by voicing nothing but dire expectations.

SENATOR FULBRIGHT: Why shouldn't we discard the objective of containing China and, despite official disclaimers, isolating her as well? Or, to state it more accurately, why shouldn't we discard a policy of helping China to isolate herself in favor of seeing what can be done to involve China in Asia—and Asia in China—and to influence China to play a constructive and stabilizing, rather than a destructive and disruptive, role in the world?

The complex problems that revolve around the words "Taiwan" and "Vietnam" will take years to unravel. In the meantime, it seems to me, everything possible should be done to clear the air—travel, trade, cultural relations. In addition, I think it would improve the atmosphere if the United States were to state clearly and unqualifiedly that this government is willing to recognize that the government of the People's Republic of China controls the mainland. The most recent statement on this subject by one of our high government officials, made in mid-1968, that "the territory controlled and administered by Peking is obviously not unknown to us" does not seem to carry quite the meaning I have in mind. There was, I felt, some grudging condescension in this formulation, the kind of condescension that the richest and most powerful nation in the world need not demonstrate.

SENATOR HATFIELD: Even if the United States abandons its isolation policy and substantially modifies its attempt at military containment, I have serious doubts that we will make much headway until we bring about a fundamental change in our attitude toward the Chinese. Until we learn to view the Chinese as people, abandon our self-righteous view that somehow we are above doing evil, and look at our conflicts as differences of opinion rather than as evidences of Chinese moral inferiority, the Chinese attitude toward us will probably remain belligerent and hostile.

MR. EZAKI: After all, the United States is the world's greatest and wealthiest nation. Why can it not have the magnanimity to teach the Chinese that there is such a thing as *Pacem in*

Terris? Nothing is as fearful as people living in ignorance. Why do we keep them out of the United Nations? Why can't we bring this vast mass of people into international society? They are communists today, sure, but they need not remain communists for all history. If we could only show them the value of freedom, if we could only show them the value of peace, then we would have a new China.

SENATOR HATFIELD: I am not so sure we would. The Chinese are determined to destroy their traditional society and cultural forms and build a "new man." Their political ideology gives meaning to their lives and to their sacrifices. Chinese commitment to ideology is probably much more profound than it would be in a society with religious traditions or one geared to satisfying material needs. Economic considerations may eventually temper Chinese ideology, but this assumption should not be made casually.

To the Chinese, their political philosophy and revolution are not a means to an end but the end itself. For this reason I consider the Chinese a greater long-term challenge to the United States than the Soviets. The Russians share our secular creed of materialistic pragmatism.

Also, the Cultural Revolution may inhibit the decline of ideology within China. It is significant, I believe, that much of China's younger generation sided with Mao in his attempt to purge society of those elements that were moderating the ideological fervor and momentum of the revolution. The role of the Red Guard has broad international implications. These young people were deeply committed to the spiritual transformation of man and society and were determined to destroy the bureaucracy they believed was inhibiting this revolution. And their ambitions and grievances are shared, in general, by all youth. This is a discomforting thought. If Mao has succeeded in nothing else, he must be given credit for being the first major government leader to exploit effectively the universal idealism of youth and their alienation from unresponsive institutions.

One further thought. Historically the Chinese have believed in the superiority of their culture. They have made little effort to impose it on others by force, assuming instead that their superiority would be appreciated and emulated. If we look at Chinese history, we will find it easier to accept the conclusion of scholars that China today has little intention of forcing her revolutionary model on others through military conquest. But if we listen only to the belligerent and militant rhetoric emanating from Peking and make no effort to place it in the context of Chinese actions in the past, we will continue to think Peking is bent on overt military aggression.

SENATOR FULBRIGHT: To date we have been very much the object of Sino-Soviet rivalry. Each of these two countries has seemed, at times, to compete in seeing which can be the more anti-American. I would think that we would much prefer to be the object of Sino-Soviet competition to see which of these two great powers could enjoy better relations with us.

"Our fate and the fate of much of the world may well turn on events in Asia, and our policy is now at a crossroads as momentous as any in our history."
Roger Hilsman

7 The Vietnam War in Perspective

STATEMENTS BY:

Munenori Akagi
John Sherman Cooper
Mark O. Hatfield
J.W. Fulbright
Shunichi Matsumoto

MUNENORI AKAGI:

The Vietnam War is not a simple clash between communism and liberal democracy. Civil strife developed in Vietnam originally from a complex variety of internal conflicts—economic, religious, and political—but great power rivalry moving against the strong force of Vietnamese nationalism has converted this war into an international struggle for domination of the Pacific.

The elements that produced the war in Vietnam are present in some measure throughout Asia. Any peace proposal must face these basic realities and work toward formulating measures to cope with them. If the Vietnam War were to be defined in Paris as the civil conflict that it basically is, the prolonged Paris conference might through negotiation create conditions that would permit American forces to withdraw.

The impasse between the Vietcong and the South Vietnamese government has its roots in the nature of the present government. Whatever the character of past governments, most of which had little to recommend them to the South Vietnamese people, the present ruling group in the south has degenerated into nothing more than an authoritarian clique run by a handful of military leaders who are completely out of touch with the people. It has suppressed all South Vietnam's neutral elements and alienated the bulk of the population. Perhaps the most effective effort the United States could make, even now, would be to apply pressure to reform the government of South Vietnam. If it were close to the people and had the will and the ability to stand on its own feet, it might be capable of taking the responsible measures necessary to end the fighting.

North Vietnam does not welcome aid from Communist China, with its implication of Chinese interference in North Vietnamese affairs. Nor is China pleased with North Vietnam's independent course. And the Soviet Union stands between the two, trying to prevent Chinese intervention and even acting as a mediator between the United States and North Vietnam.

These are some of the realities the negotiators must face if they are to cope with the dangerous situation in Southeast Asia today.

JOHN SHERMAN COOPER:

In my judgment, the war in Vietnam is the clearest expression of America's containment policy in Asia. When the American people began questioning our government's course in Vietnam, they challenged, in effect, the validity of the containment policy itself.

The Vietnam War and the protests against it have had profound and far-reaching effects in the United States. The political career of one President has foundered on the problems this conflict engendered, and the new President cannot be immune to its effects. Public reaction has, in some instances, gone so far as to demand the pullback of American troops from all of Asia and the abandonment of United States bases there. The Executive and the Congress have no choice but to read the lessons of the past in charting our course for the future.

Just as the war itself has forced us to consider a new direction, or at least a new emphasis, in our foreign policy, the settlement we finally reach could be the turning point in our relations with the countries of Asia. Any settlement, to be effective, must have the acceptance of China as well as of the immediate parties to the conflict. Indeed, Communist China, supported by North Vietnam, may insist on direct participation in the talks as the price of her coöperation in upholding an eventual settlement.

If China should, through her participation and coöperation, help to insure an end to fighting and a beginning of stability in Southeast Asia, we would, I believe, have the essential elements of a new relationship among the Pacific powers. China's influence and position in Asia would be assured. An independent Vietnam, with a government chosen by the people, and the reassured countries of Laos, Cambodia, and Thailand could at last deal autonomously with both the East and the West. In such circumstances the United States might be emboldened to try withdrawing its Seventh Fleet from the Quemoy Straits to lessen hostility. With measures like these, we might gradually move from a policy of containment to a policy of coöperation and healthy competition in Asia.

MARK O. HATFIELD:

When he took over in the White House, Mr. Nixon inherited a set of unpleasant realities in Vietnam, in Paris, and at home. Thirty thousand Americans had died on the battlefield, and casualties were mounting at the rate of 150 to two hundred a week; the stalemated Paris talks were confined largely to an exchange of recriminations; and the American public was still remembering former Secretary Rusk's demogogic appeals for support in combating the Yellow Peril of China, which he identified as the real demon behind our enemy in Vietnam.

Mr. Nixon had pledged to wind up the war in Vietnam and win the peace in Asia. The ugly realities he faced could persuade him to move in one of two directions.

Strong elements in the United States continued to believe not only that we were losing the Vietnam War because we have tied the hands of our military but also that an all-out military effort could still salvage a victory for America. In late 1966, when our bombers were attacking targets twenty-five miles from the Chinese border, we heard some voices urging the Administration then to do the job it must ultimately do—bomb Peking. Those of this persuasion may have been lying low during the Presidential race but there was no reason to believe they had disappeared. Mr. Nixon was privately urged to wind up the war by bombing Vietnam back into the Stone Age.

In the alternative effort to negotiate American troops away from Asian soil, only one real question has faced the negotiators in Paris: the time and the method of American withdrawal from Vietnam and the mainland of Asia. Allowing for face-saving embellishments and transitional steps, I think this has always been the single issue.

Peace cannot be the mere absence of war. We in the United States need to develop a sense of urgency about laying true foundations for a lasting peace. While we are seeking solutions to the present conflict, let us not erect obstacles to block the peace of the future. Let us avoid the pitfalls of bigger and better missile systems and be vigilant to the growing danger of the military-industrial-academic complex in this country.

The foundations of peace are understanding, knowledge, and the absence of fear. On these foundations America must build confidence in the authenticity of our policy. Thanks to the transistor radio, what America is and what America does is known in all of its definitive terms and its contradictions to remote villagers in every part of the world. To bring validity to our actions, we must dissipate the mystique of violence that surrounds our policies both at home and abroad. If we do, perhaps we can replace the fear that permeates our thinking today with love in a true Judeo-Christian sense. As St. John has said, "Where there is fear there is something imperfect in your love."

J.W. FULBRIGHT:

I do not doubt that the Peking government would like to see the United States defeated in Vietnam and a communist or pro-communist regime installed there. I am sure that Peking would prefer sympathetic to hostile states surrounding China, just as we prefer sympathetic governments in the Western Hemisphere. China would also undoubtedly like to see wars of national liberation succeed, just as we would like to see them fail. Peking obviously desires the removal of American military power from Southeast Asia, feeling—rightly or wrongly—that the American presence there threatens her directly. I would venture to guess that as long as there is a massive American military presence in Southeast Asia on the scale that now exists, progress toward accommodation with China will be difficult.

I do not mean to imply that progress can result only from an American defeat in Vietnam. After all, China has been willing to accept compromise settlements in Southeast Asia before, in Geneva in 1954 and again in 1962 at the conference on Laos.

The 1954 Geneva Agreements banned the introduction of fresh troops, military personnel, armaments, munitions, and foreign military bases into Vietnam, Cambodia, and Laos; and they restricted the participation of these three states in military alliances. In the Final Declaration of the Geneva Conference, the members of the conference, including the People's Republic of China, agreed "to respect the sovereignty, the independence, the unity, and the territorial integrity" of Cambodia, Laos, and Vietnam and "to refrain from any interference in their internal affairs." The 1954 Geneva Agreements thus seem to me to amount to neutralization of this area, in fact if not in name.

The 1962 conference on Laos resulted in a specific "Declaration of the Neutrality of Laos." The parties to the conference—again including the People's Republic of China—declared that they would respect the neutrality of the Kingdom of Laos, would not bring Laos into any military alliances "inconsistent with her neutrality," and would not introduce foreign troops into, or establish foreign military installations in, that country.

I see no reason to assume that the Chinese would not again accept a compromise settlement in Southeast Asia if, regardless of the character of the government in Vietnam, the settlement provided that Vietnam would be neutralized and that no foreign bases or forces would remain there. We ourselves have declared our willingness to withdraw all our forces from Vietnam, implicitly by referring to the Geneva Agreements of 1954 as an acceptable basis for settlement and explicitly in the Manila Conference communiqué.

If the stage is reached in the negotiations when parties other than those who began the process in Paris will be asked to participate or if the negotiations are extended to relate to countries other than Vietnam, I believe that mainland China should be invited to be present. Without Chinese coöperation, no settlement can remain in force for long.

SHUNICHI MATSUMOTO:

With prospects for an end to the war in Vietnam growing brighter, a policy aimed at neutralizing Southeast Asia is gaining favor not only in the United States but in many other areas of the world. While this solution attracts wide support in the abstract, few concrete measures have been considered, and strong doubt persists that neutralization of the region will ever materialize. The gap between abstract approval and pragmatic implementation is nowhere more evident than in Southeast Asia itself. There, a growing feeling of regional solidarity, and the desire to escape the international power struggle, conflicts with a natural anxiety about the effects of American withdrawal from the area.

Many Japanese have assumed that neutralization of Southeast Asia would mean the simultaneous neutralization of Japan. Many have, therefore, tended to resent the concept.

Neutralization was once a revolutionary proposal. In March, 1966, Senator Fulbright startled his colleagues by suggesting that the United States should seek to neutralize the whole of Southeast Asia in order to effect a reconciliation with China. Since then such influential figures as United Nations Secretary-General U Thant and Sir Anthony Eden, former British Foreign Secretary, have strongly advocated the concept introduced by Senator Fulbright.

Both Chinese and Indian cultural influence is strong throughout Southeast Asia, but the nations of this area belong to neither sphere. Vietnam resisted active Chinese encroachment for one thousand years and was the only country to feel severe pressure from the People's Middle Kingdom. Historically, China's heart has been in the central reaches of the Yellow River, and her concern has focused on the nomadic tribes of northern Asia, which threatened to encroach upon this region, and on the peoples to her west, whose culture was far different from her own.

China's attitude toward the nations to the south and east has historically shown none of the concern exhibited toward her northern and western neighbors. One of America's most significant errors in its assessment of events in Vietnam has been to misjudge China's aggressive intentions in Southeast Asia. It has considered North Vietnam and, indirectly, the National Liberation Front, as puppets of the People's Republic of China; by applying the logic of the Cold War to Asian developments, it has blinded itself to the reality of rising nationalism.

The lesson of Vietnam is quite clearly that the United States cannot ensure stability in any country by supplying unilateral military support to a government unable to control rebellious elements within its own sphere. The United States may consider only two courses in the future if it wishes to avoid another Vietnam. One is the neutralization of former French Indochina; the other, a Pacific security structure embracing the non-communist Asian nations, led by Japan.

Mr. Nixon has proposed a new security arrangement that would give the friendly Pacific countries more direct responsibility for their own mutual defense. He suggested that SEATO and other reciprocal aid treaties be replaced by an organization in which Japan would play the predominant role, with the indirect support of United States military might. It appears that he was proposing to convert one of the existing organizations, like ASPAC, into a military alliance and at the same time to strengthen Japan's defense system.

Such a security system cannot materialize, for it ignores the hopes and fears of the Asian peoples. If, by some remote chance, it were to go into effect, it could only create greater misunderstandings and perhaps involve the United States more deeply than ever in tragic wars of containment. Both Japan and the countries of Southeast Asia oppose turning ASPAC or any other existing organization into a military alliance. And should Japan take a position of military leadership in any Pacific security structure, the people of Asia would immediately resurrect memories of the Greater East Asia Co-Prosperity Sphere and the oppressive events of World War II.

Neutralization of Vietnam, Laos, and Cambodia, therefore, remains the only realistic alternative. At this stage the Philippines, Thailand, Malaysia, Singapore, Burma, and Indonesia, with their own special circumstances and individual problems, might find it difficult to join the Indochinese countries in one large, neutral structure. All but two of these nations already follow largely independent, neutral policies.

Now, as before, any policy aimed at neutralization, whether it is extended to include all of Southeast Asia or limited to former French Indochina, can be no more than a scrap of paper without the coöperation of the Communist Chinese. The issue reverts once more to the problem of persuading mainland China to rejoin the international community. I would not consider it unrealistic to expect China to act as a guarantor of Southeast Asian neutrality if the United States were to modify its "Stop-China" policy. In the last analysis, the stability of Southeast Asia is in American hands. The United States, and the United States alone, can take the initiative.

III

THE CRITICAL QUESTIONS: A TIME FOR ENTRENCHMENT OR AN OPPORTUNITY FOR MODIFICATION?

''The dogmas of the quiet past are
inadequate to the stormy present. The
occasion is piled high with difficulty, and we
must rise with the occasion. As our case is
new, so must we think anew and act anew.
We must disenthrall ourselves ''
Abraham Lincoln

It is the United States of America in the year, 1969. Ten thousand Chinese military personnel are billeted on Long Island, and another Chinese contingent maintains a base on Hawaii. Off the shores of California and in the Atlantic from New York to Florida, the Polaris submarines of the People's Republic patrol ceaselessly back and forth. Planes based on Long Island, bearing the Communist star, appear suddenly over inland cities and towns, making casual observations. Meanwhile, the American Ambassador to the United Nations waits outside, barred from his seat by the power of the Chinese contingent

Americans attending the Pacem in Terris II *conference in Geneva, Switzerland, in 1967 were startled to hear such a description of the United States in a role it has never experienced. The speaker was Paul T.K. Lin, a Canadian, who is an associate professor of history at McGill University. From the early days of the People's Republic until 1964, he taught Chinese history, international law, and international relations at Hua Chiao University in China. He was asking the Americans in his audience to place themselves in Chinese shoes for one brief moment.*

105

Since 1949, China's perspective on international affairs has necessarily been far different from that of the United States. Whereas the country inherited by Mao Tse-tung had achieved some degree of modernization in education, transportation, public health, commerce and banking, and many other fields, it was also a land in disarray. The nation suffered from starvation, unemployment, dislocation, and inflation, and the people, especially the peasants, nursed fresh memories of oppression, terror, and tyranny. Finally in undisputed control and faced with the results of more than a century of depression and disunion, the communist regime hoped for a respite from foreign pressures so that it might devote full attention to the needs of the homeland.

One of Mao's first foreign-policy statements, made just prior to the proclamation of the People's Republic, expressed his willingness to "discuss with any foreign government the establishment of diplomatic relations on the basis of the principles of equality, mutual benefit, and mutual respect for territorial integrity and sovereignty." His only conditions were that Chinese affairs be left to Chinese to settle and that foreign powers cease to conspire with Chinese reactionaries.

The Western powers, not yet adjusted to the reality that colonialism was a thing of the past and startled by the collapse of Chiang's foreign-backed forces, responded with predictable negativism. Winston Churchill described Mao's ascendance as *"the worst disaster suffered by the West since the war." From the start, the communist regime faced a powerful anti-Chinese propaganda campaign abroad, chiefly from the United States. This campaign intensified after the Korean War.*

Chinese foreign policy has had both long-term and immediate objectives. In Mao Tse-tung's own terms, the ultimate goal is "a new world of permanent peace and permanent light," accomplished through "proletarian internationalism." In short, the international vision of the followers of Mao is a truly communist world to supplant the existing international power structure. As the Chinese see it, the means of accomplishing this goal is indigenous revolution on the Chinese model, carried out by the oppressed peoples of the world.

China's short-term objectives bring her into conflict with the current policies of other powers, notably the United States and the Soviet Union. China is unyielding in her determination to preserve her national identity and to resist any form of foreign interference. Freedom from interference implies freedom to trade. China desires redress for her century of humiliation in the form of worldwide recognition as one of the great powers. Considerable evidence indicates that the Chinese effort to attain nuclear capacity has as its ultimate aim the right to claim diplomatic as well as military equality with the two superpowers. Perhaps her most frequently

*repeated objective is the removal of the
United States military presence from East
and Southeast Asia, particularly from
Taiwan, and the establishment of a
Chinese sphere of influence. And finally,
as a step toward the ultimate unlimited
goal, China aspires to dominance in the
socialist world as the one true example of
pure revolutionary rule, an ambition that
runs counter to the traditional role of the
U.S.S.R.*

*China's view of the world, and her own
role in it, has been conditioned by her
prewar experience with Western
expansionism and by her frustration at
the continuing hostility of the West in the
postwar era. When the United States and
its allies speak of "maintaining the
peace," China, in the light of her
particular experience, can interpret the
term only as "maintaining the threat."*

*"No equilibrium is stable as long as the
forces tending to disrupt it are unrecognized
or ignored."*
Sir Mark L.E. Oliphant

8   Security for East and West

A DISCUSSION WITH:

Edwin O. Reischauer
Aiichiro Fujiyama
Fred Warner Neal
Elisabeth Mann Borgese
Don Edwards
Munenori Akagi
Masumi Ezaki
J.W. Fulbright
Arthur Goldberg
John Sherman Cooper
Stanley Sheinbaum
Alan Cranston
Tokuma Utsunomiya
Kazuo Shionoya

AMBASSADOR REISCHAUER: In the nineteen-fifties Americans pictured a world divided in two—half communist, half non-communist. As the foremost nation in the free world, the United States led the struggle to man the dikes against the tide of communism, fearful that it might flood the vulnerable lowlands of the non-communist world. We were particularly concerned about the weak areas in underdeveloped Asia.

Today Americans are finding that our picture of the world was faulty. As the Japanese discovered in China and the Soviets have more recently learned in both Asia and Europe, nationalism is the strongest current sweeping over emerging nations today. Where nationalism flourishes, its force frustrates outside control of any kind. The United States is the latest country to appreciate its power.

If we are not able to control events in Vietnam, we may be certain that the Chinese cannot do it either. With an improved understanding of our error in judgment in Southeast Asia will come a reassessment of the value of our containment policy toward China. I believe that the United States will adjust its position to take a more reasonable approach, one that will reduce pressure on the Chinese and will worry the Japanese somewhat less than at present.

We must realize that "containment" means different things to Americans and Japanese. To us it stands for the discouragement or prevention of aggression. The Japanese translation of containment, *fujikome,* unfortunately carries an aggressive rather than a defensive connotation; it means "a blockade" or "a bottling up." Misunderstanding can therefore arise merely from our interpretation of the term.

MR. FUJIYAMA: It may be, as Ambassador Reischauer says, that the Japanese translation of containment is inaccurate. From what we have seen of the practical application of United

States policy, however, perhaps *fujikome* is the proper word after all. American troops in the Far East may not be intended for offense, but their very presence supports the Japanese interpretation that the United States is bottling up China. The misunderstanding is not merely semantic, I believe; it arises also from the divergence between the mild American term and its pragmatic consequences.

AMBASSADOR REISCHAUER: Mr. Fujiyama is quite right in picking me up, and I am in complete agreement that our formidable military presence in Asia should be reduced in the interest of a better relationship with China. We should remove two strong irritants to the Chinese: our Okinawan nuclear arsenal and our bases on Taiwan. Neither is especially consequential to our defense. These would be the first steps toward abandonment of the close-in containment that arouses Chinese animosity. China's internal interests and weaknesses, coupled with the strength of her neighbors, contain her more adequately than can American advance bases, nuclear or conventional.

PROFESSOR NEAL: Would you say that the American military presence in Thailand creates a problem with China?

AMBASSADOR REISCHAUER: I don't think it's a direct problem in our relationship with China, but it does have some implications. Personally, I feel that we should not have bases in Thailand or anywhere else in that region. If we withdrew them, perhaps we might make a slight contribution toward improving the China situation.

Let me add at this point that Americans also have trouble with that word containment. It has a double meaning. All too often we think of containment as containment-with-isolation—banning trade, isolating China from international society, and preventing intercourse of any kind. Isolation is not necessarily a part of containment; containment *without isolation* is the interpretation we should consider.

MRS. BORGESE: How can we, on one hand, favor coexistence with China by expanding trade and cultural exchange and on the other hand insist on a course of military containment? The two approaches seem to be completely contradictory.

MR. FUJIYAMA: If we look at the picture from the other side, withdrawal of troops alone will not erase the threat of China in the Far East. We should invite China into the United Nations, undertake cultural exchange, and try to develop ties that will lead to eventual recognition. If we were to work in these directions, the so-called Chinese threat would diminish and friendly relations between the United States and China would ensue.

MR. EDWARDS: All the reëvaluations that Japan and the countries of the West might make regarding the political, economic, and social isolation of China are not going to be relevant until we find answers to questions of security, around which our military containment policy revolves.

MRS. BORGESE: I see obvious parallels between the American position in Western Europe and its attitude toward the Soviet Union and the American position on East Asian security and its attitude toward the People's Republic of China. Both were originally based primarily on containment and encirclement of what was presumed to be the aggressive expansionism of a monolithic world-communist movement. Both were implemented in the course of the economic and political reconstruction of defeated enemy nations.

In Europe isolation following World War I, and containment following World War II, were more or less abandoned when it turned out that world communism was not monolithic, that Soviet power was introverted rather than expansionist, and that active coexistence was not only possible but inevitable. Whether this evolution was subjective or objective, that is, whether the reality changed or merely our perception of it, is a secondary question. The important point is that this evolution has left our Atlantic security structure in disarray, has alienated France, and is altering the internal political balance of power among the Western European nations. The Czechoslovak crisis has not essentially altered these prevalent trends.

The changing role of China, or our changing perception of it, is bound to induce analogous changes in East Asia. However, there are basic differences that make the situation there far more explosive than that in Western Europe.

The concept of containment, which at least *seemed* to work in Europe during the early postwar period, was transposed ready-made, so to speak, to an area where even the appearance of workability could not be attained. As Senator Eugene McCarthy pointed out in his book, *The Limits of Power,* in Europe the United States was confronted with a system of traditional nations, albeit in a state of transition and transformation, while "Southeast Asia is not a complex of nation-states but a rather generalized, undifferentiated world.' And Senator Fulbright has warned us that "China is a society and a civilization, not a nation-state in the Western sense." Our NATO allies, at least in the beginning, had military weight and political substance, but our SEATO alliance has been shunned from the start by the major Asian powers and has remained essentially non-Asian.

In Europe it was a defeated power, Germany, that was divided; in Asia it was China, a wartime ally. The Soviet Union can much more easily accommodate to a divided Germany—insisting only that its own client, the German Democratic Republic, be recognized—than China can acquiesce to the division of her own territory and people.

Considering Japan's impressive rate of industrial and social development and the depressed, underdeveloped, and chaotic state of many countries in East Asia, Japan might play a role in the reconstruction and development of the region similar to the part Israel could take in the development of the surrounding Arab countries, among which she enjoys a similarly privileged and contrasting position. But both countries, with their ties to the United States military-industrial complex, may be prevented from playing such a constructive role as long as they are "outposts of Western imperialism," seen by the communist bloc as barriers to the general neutralization of the areas, a *sine qua non* for the establishment of peace.

MR. AKAGI: Like Mr. Fujiyama, I believe that raising the

114

standard of living throughout Asia would be the surest and most effective way of erecting a wall against communist penetration. But, with Mrs. Borgese, I think that until America's military containment policy is relaxed, it is impossible to advance these other positive measures. American military commitments to nations on the continent of Asia serve to intensify confrontations and prevent solutions to the overriding problems of divided countries.

A nation is a nation, regardless of whether it is communist or free. We cannot ignore the existence of a country nor can we expel it from the ranks of international society. And we cannot achieve security by placing our confidence in military might alone.

Before we can achieve the long-term measures Mr. Fujiyama advocates, America must gradually eliminate its land bases in the Pacific. I do not think that an immediate withdrawal, particularly from Southeast Asia, would be wise at present. With the vacuum that such a sudden pullback would create, Southeast Asia might present a tempting target for communist aggression. Should the Strait of Malacca ever be closed, Japan's entire economy would grind to a halt. At the present stage the United States should shift its emphasis from land bases to sea power and maintain a strong defense with its Seventh Fleet. The most powerful submarines in the world, equipped with Polaris missiles, could guarantee the security of Asia while land bases are gradually phased out.

MR. FUJIYAMA: From a broad standpoint, the Seventh Fleet is necessary for the security of Asia, but how do the Chinese regard the Seventh Fleet? When Mr. Kenzo Matsumura, one of our party elders, went to China recently to meet with Chou En-lai and Foreign Minister Chen-yi, he found that the biggest problem between the United States and China is the presence of the Seventh Fleet in the Straits of Taiwan. From his conversations, Mr. Matsumura got the clear impression that the Chinese are afraid of the Seventh Fleet. To relax tension, the Seventh Fleet should be assigned the broader mission of patrolling Asian waters so that the Chinese will not have the impression that its single purpose is to defend the Straits of Taiwan against them.

MR. EZAKI: The Chinese are very sensitive to any matter connected with Taiwan, but they are almost equally sensitive to the United States nuclear base on Okinawa. Perhaps American and Japanese militarists derive comfort and satisfaction from having a missile base there, but it irritates China and it incenses many Japanese. In my opinion, this nuclear base serves no significant security purpose that could not be achieved equally well by the Polaris submarines of the Seventh Fleet. If the nuclear base were removed from Okinawa, China would at least have evidence of America's good intentions.

MR. AKAGI: There is really no need to store strategic nuclear weapons on or transfer tactical nuclear arms to Okinawa. Japan is protected by the so-called nuclear umbrella of the United States. Strategic nuclear weapons in the hands of a single nation provide no deterrent, as the bombing of Hiroshima and Nagasaki has proved. But with two major powers, the United States and the Soviet Union, both having massive nuclear capacity, we do have mutual deterrence. Advance nuclear bases do not increase the deterrent factor, and tactical nuclear weapons cannot be used in combat without the danger of sparking a major holocaust. Removal of U.S. nuclear weapons to rear bases in the Marianas would in no sense diminish the American capacity to retaliate, and conventional bases both on Okinawa and in South Korea would be sufficient to handle any crisis that develops.

SENATOR FULBRIGHT: May I ask you a question? What is the attitude of the Japanese toward the American proposal to build an anti-ballistic-missile system?

MR. AKAGI: The ABM is meant as a defense against Russia, and I believe that it is necessary to the United States. The development of the ABM is a U.S. military problem and we cannot criticize it, but we believe that the United States should devote more of its efforts toward preventing a major war.

SENATOR FULBRIGHT: With all deference, this ABM was

justified in our Congress as a defense against China's nuclear weapons, not Russia's.

MR. AKAGI: China's development of nuclear weapons is not for offensive purposes, and it will be more than ten years before China's nuclear capacity can be classed as a war deterrent force. If the ABM is directed against China, then I think it is not necessary. If the ABM is intended to deter Russia, then I believe it is essential.

AMBASSADOR GOLDBERG: Speaking of Russia, can Japan and the United States be friendly both to China and to the Soviet Union at the same time?

MR. EZAKI: The policy of peaceful coexistence between the United States and the Soviet Union, resulting in a thaw in the Cold War, was a significant historical development brought about by the efforts of Khrushchev and the late President Kennedy. But today, when the Soviet Union has become China's greatest enemy, peaceful coexistence between Russia and the United States takes on the connotation of collusion in the containment of China. I feel that any such collaboration would be a mistake. Is there any reason for the United States to side with Soviet Russia in containing China? If United States-Soviet peaceful coexistence is possible, United States-Chinese coexistence should be even easier to achieve.

The problem is China's tendency to seal herself off from outside contacts. United States policies have helped to drive China into her hard shell. By the same token, America can help China to break out by easing its containment policy. Soviet-American collaboration against China, on the other hand, would not advance Asian security and would certainly prevent Sino-American peaceful coexistence.

SENATOR COOPER: If the Japanese pleas for the removal of American nuclear bases and the gradual withdrawal of American troops from all of Asia were to be carried into effect, we would have a major modification in our present policy of containment. The President of the United States, as a Republican, has a great opportunity to adjust our policy, and he will be influenced, I would think, by Japanese attitudes.

Do the statements made here by my Japanese colleagues represent the policy of their government? Would the measures you suggest be acceptable to your government? Would they be acceptable to your people? If so, they might have a significant effect on future United States Asian policy.

MR. EZAKI: The majority of the people of Japan support the views expressed here. Japan's Socialist Party takes an anti-American, pro-Chinese stand, but members of the Liberal Democratic Party, representing a much more predominant popular opinion, for the most part support continued Japanese-United States friendship together with the development of a more coöperative relationship with China. The official Japanese government position, I believe, does not reflect the majority opinion in Japan on China policy, although it may still draw majority support from within the Liberal Democratic Party. The government, I am afraid, feels it must not irritate the United States. As the United States moves forward to a more conciliatory stance, the Japanese government will move ahead more positively also, particularly if members of the Liberal Democratic Party who feel as we do exert pressure for a new policy.

MR. AKAGI: The present Japanese government supports and coöperates in America's containment policy. This joint stand reminds me of one of Aesop's fables about the contest between the sun and the wind. The harder the wind blew, the tighter the traveler wrapped his coat around him, but in the warmth of the sun, he took it off immediately. In Vietnam the United States has been blowing with all its military might, but the North Vietnamese have responded by wrapping their cloak of determination more tightly around them. Never will the strong wind of American military power divest China of her hostility. Only under the warmth of a generous American and Japanese desire to help the less fortunate peoples of Asia will China come to shed her defensive posture.

THE TREATY OF MUTUAL
COÖPERATION AND SECURITY

AMBASSADOR REISCHAUER: The United States and Japan depend on each other far more than either country quite realizes. Both countries take their relationship for granted, giving little thought to what might happen if the Japanese-American partnership came to an abrupt end.

The United States is in a time of crisis in its relationship with Japan, and a misunderstanding over China contributes to this crisis. The Security Treaty, ratified with such difficulty and commotion in 1960, extends only until June 23, 1970. At that time either side can denounce it, and, on one year's notice, the treaty will go out of being. Those groups in Japan opposed to the Japanese-American relationship have aimed at 1970 as the year to break the tie between our two countries. We can expect a steady buildup of excitement and political turmoil in Japan between now and then.

Three major problems, if left unresolved, will endanger the vastly important mutual relationship between Japan and the United States. The first is Vietnam, where the Japanese see Americans bogged down in a repetition of their own story in China during the thirties. Many Japanese are terrified that, because of their close military ties to America, they will be dragged into an awful war against the Chinese, and possibly against the Russians. For this reason alone, I think it imperative that the Vietnam War be well on its way to termination before 1970.

The second source of difficulty is the status of Okinawa. Approximately one million Japanese have lived in an American military colony for twenty-four years, the only colony set up since the Second World War. This unsound situation between two major allies should be resolved before it gets mixed up with the Security Treaty question.

The third issue is the whole problem of the respective Japanese and American attitudes and actions toward China.

Japan's relative position in the international economic world is by no means static. As nearly as can be estimated, Japan had two-thirds the G.N.P. of China in 1960; today Japan's gross national product is one and a half times that of China, and Japan has only about one-seventh of China's population. Before the decade is out, or soon thereafter, Japan will be as big in economic terms as China, India, and all the rest of Asia combined, including the oil-rich lands of West Asia.

As a major Asian power, Japan will have far greater interest than the United States in the development of East Asia, in rewarding relations with the Chinese, and in a peaceful atmosphere in the Pacific. Therefore the major responsibility for deciding what part each of our countries will play in the Asia of the future should fall to the Japanese. What is a useful American military role in the western Pacific? How can we best coördinate our economic efforts in that part of the world? How can we best approach the Chinese problem?

I am suggesting that, as we go into the nineteen-seventies, Americans and Japanese should make a great effort to change the dominant image we have held of a Japanese-American relationship based on a time when the United States occupied Japan. We must come to realize that in East Asia we are partners; we share the same basic goals and have the same fundamental interests. In determining what we should do and how we should do it in future years, Japan will be the senior partner and America, the junior partner.

MR. SHEINBAUM: One thing that disturbs me, Mr. Ambassador, is your description of Japanese-American interdependence as being primarily military. I wonder if there is not more to interdependence than that.

AMBASSADOR REISCHAUER: The point is well taken. The military problem is the difficult issue, the one that is most debated, but obviously our economic and cultural relationship is by far the most important. Next to that comes our interdependence in the problems of helping technologically and economically less-developed countries to advance. And only third, at most, would be the military issue.

As we in the United States move from one concept of our purpose in Asia to another, we may overreact. One great danger is that we may pull completely out of the western Pacific, isolating ourselves from the less-developed parts of the world. I think the United States has a continuing, useful military role but a limited one. By maintaining the Seventh Fleet in the Far Pacific, along with certain of our alliances, we would have a potential for responding to overt aggression. We could thus inhibit real disturbances and make a contribution to the external stability of the area. Internal stability is a different matter; there, I think we cannot contribute substantially.

Our presence in Asian waters would assure freedom of the seas and guarantee the lines of communication on which the Japanese industrial machine depends. In Korea I think we do have the danger of war breaking out if it is not made clear that we will guarantee the security of South Korea. Our ability to inhibit overt aggression in Asia would serve Japanese interests more than it would serve American.

PROFESSOR NEAL: If the United States were to withdraw to the central Pacific, exactly what harm might come to Japan? I have some general idea, but what precisely would happen? China, we are told, will not invade anyone. Ambassador Reischauer says something unfortunate will happen in Korea, but I am not quite sure what it is. Would anything else take place to affect either the United States or Japan?

AMBASSADOR REISCHAUER: I think the greatest specific danger would arise in Korea where two tough regimes are eager to conquer each other. The Pueblo incident and many other more serious events illustrate the tension there. A withdrawal of the American commitment to South Korea would, I think, be likely to lead to a resumption of large-scale warfare in Korea, and this in turn would seriously endanger Japan's interests.

Another type of incident might be one like the ridiculous confrontation between Indonesia and Malaysia. Because we and the British had power in that part of the world, this confrontation was prevented from becoming a large-scale invasion or an effort to blockade trade routes.

If there were no power at all in the Far East, any adventurer like Sukarno could easily block the Japanese oil lines with catastrophic results. All of these examples, except for the Korean one, may seem a little farfetched, but if the Japanese people suddenly sensed that they were alone in their part of the world, I feel certain they would rush toward rearmament. I think the Japanese-American Treaty really saves them from what they fear most, a return to arms. Japanese rearmament would cause grave problems domestically and alarm her neighbors. It would divert Japanese interest away from economic aid to underdeveloped countries. And if we were to pull back to the mid-Pacific, our already dwindling aid programs would shrink even further.

PROFESSOR NEAL: So there would be two things: the possibility of local wars that could expand and the likelihood of Japanese rearmament?

AMBASSADOR REISCHAUER: Yes, rearmament, probably going all the way to nuclear weapons, and with it the greatest possible danger for both Japan and the United States. Japanese and American experts agree that the only grave danger Japan could face in the foreseeable future would be a hostile United States; for us, a hostile Japan would be the only serious threat in all of Asia. If both countries were militarized and headed on different courses, enmity between the two could readily emerge once more.

AMBASSADOR GOLDBERG: Why should we have a more peaceful world with the United States acting as the policeman for Japan instead of Japan acting as her own policeman? The logic of what you have said, Ambassador, is that we must maintain a large military establishment to keep the peace of Asia and to keep open the trade routes to Japan. Why does it make for a more peaceful world to have the great military power of the United States become even greater? Why isn't it more logical for the smaller countries to assume the responsibility, especially if Japan is to become the senior partner, as you say?

AMBASSADOR REISCHAUER: You are making me sound like a real militarist. I am describing a greatly *reduced* American role and one that the Japanese help us to define. We will certainly maintain at least some degree of military force in mid-Pacific in any case. I think it would be unproductive for us to keep up an effective level of power in mid-Pacific while the Japanese maintain forces at a similar level, as a substitute for our Seventh Fleet, in the western Pacific. Also, the Japanese have specific political problems at this time. I think they do not wish to trust themselves with remilitarizing, and I know their neighbors would be upset. If the United States were to play a limited military role throughout the Pacific, we would have a more peaceful world, with less military expenditure, than if we withdrew to mid-Pacific and the Japanese took over the military role in the western Pacific.

PROFESSOR NEAL: Would people in Asia distrust the Japanese more than they distrust us? After all, many people don't trust us very far.

AMBASSADOR REISCHAUER: Quite frankly, I cannot imagine anyone in Asia who doesn't trust us more in military affairs than they do the Japanese, including the Chinese. The Koreans, the Filipinos, the Thais—all would trust the United States militarily more than they would trust Japan.

MRS. BORGESE: Once more I sense a basic contradiction. All of this discussion concerns unilateral security arrangements—the American Navy replacing the British Navy or the Japanese Navy of the past. But America has a commitment to collective security, which would suggest alternative courses.

AMBASSADOR REISCHAUER: But we have a commitment to South Korea also, and I believe the American presence there serves a useful purpose. Let me clarify once more. I am *not* in favor of United States military bases in any less-developed Asian countries, with the single exception of Korea. Even there, our presence needs Japanese support. Except for Korea, I think America can maintain bases safely only in Japan.

SENATOR CRANSTON: How strong is Japanese sentiment for a change in their constitution and a reversion to large military defenses? Would the Japanese favor taking their defense into their own hands rather than relying on the United States and our nuclear umbrella or on international approaches to security?

MR. AKAGI: I do not believe that Japan needs any major military force. The present Self-Defense Force has reached the stage where it is becoming effective, and a third program of expansion is now underway. In the future we cannot take over the defense of the Asian area from the United States, but we can certainly assume responsibility for Japan's own defense.

MR. EZAKI: Any future war in Asia will in all likelihood be a conventional war. As Mr. Akagi has pointed out, the deterrent of American and Soviet nuclear capacity will probably rule out atomic warfare. Japan's own defense force, thanks to American help, has reached the stage where it can cope with any conventional threat.

Although I do not refute the value of the Japanese-American security pact, I feel that Japan is now capable of standing on her own feet. The United States should at least be willing to experiment with cutting Japan's defense force loose from American supervision without saying, like a parent to a child, "Let's wait until you have proved that you are strong enough to be independent."

Senator Cranston has asked about the Japanese attitude toward the American nuclear umbrella. Many of us feel that it is childish to talk about placing yourself under an umbrella. What umbrella? If the time should ever come when Communist China showers us with atomic bombs, would the Japanese-American Security Treaty help us? Of if the Soviets attacked Japan, would the United States come to our aid? I doubt it.

AMBASSADOR REISCHAUER: I cannot imagine the Soviets or Chinese attacking Japan without its developing into a major nuclear holocaust. We would *have* to respond. I disagree completely with Mr. Ezaki that the United States would, or could, ignore a Soviet or Chinese attack on Japan.

AMBASSADOR GOLDBERG: I agree that it's inconceivable that we would not respond to *any* nuclear attack on Japan. But putting aside the nuclear aspects for the moment, Mr. Ezaki has asked that America cut Japan loose and let her manage her own defense. But he also says, "I do not refute the Security Treaty." Always I find this reservation, this inconsistency. The Security Treaty, to be implemented, requires an American presence in Japan. And the Seventh Fleet, if it is to operate in the area, physically requires Japanese bases. We could not maintain our obligations under the treaty from so great a distance as Hawaii.

What is the Japanese position? Does Japan want protection from the Seventh Fleet, based in Japan, or is she willing to stand on her own feet under her present constitution without American protection and without rearming herself? We have an American expression, "You can't have your cake and eat it." I think the saying applies here.

MR. EZAKI: We, as a group, advocate the continuation of the United States-Japan Security Treaty and regard the Seventh Fleet as a useful deterrent force in Asia. We feel that its mobility and flexibility should be used to the utmost in discouraging and inhibiting trouble. Korea is a threat, and the Japanese regard the dispute there with great concern.

What the Japanese overwhelmingly oppose is nuclear land bases, particularly the base on Okinawa. The strategic nuclear weapons on Okinawa are aimed at China. If the Seventh Fleet, with its Polaris submarines, is used as a mobile deterrent on a broad front in the Pacific, nuclear land bases lose their utility, but they remain an irritant to China.

MR. AKAGI: Ambassador Reischauer mentioned that there is more to the Okinawan question than the nuclear bases there. Neither the Cairo nor the Potsdam declarations stipulated the American occupation of Okinawa, but these islands have been under American control since the end of the Pacific war. The San Francisco Peace Treaty recognized Japan's residual sovereignty over the Ryukyus. Unless Okinawa is returned to Japan soon, Okinawans and Japanese may become increasingly alienated from one another. To delay Okinawa's return to Japan is to suppress the aspirations of both peoples, with a resulting impairment of U.S.-Japanese friendship and the encouragement of anti-Americanism in both countries.

MR. UTSUNOMIYA: Most Japanese think the United States-Japanese Treaty is necessary for the security of Japan, but opposition to it is increasing rapidly. The kind of collective security envisioned by this treaty is becoming increasingly suspect among the Japanese. History has taught them that if world order must be maintained by arms, their security is always fragile. Japanese in overwhelming numbers still support the prohibition against rearmament in their constitution. Most regard the defense pact as a necessary evil, not as an ideal. Ambassador Reischauer has been realistic in his analyses, but the Japanese have had unfortunate experience with realistic interpretations of history. They are much more attracted to an idealistic interpretation of current affairs. Are there not many Americans who would prefer to consider the alternatives? Should we not concentrate on altering the conditions that make the Japanese-American Security Treaty necessary?

MRS. BORGESE: I wonder what *is* a realistic interpretation of history. Ambassador Reischauer's remarks on containment and on Japanese-American security leave me with the impression of a paradox. The Japan that he has convincingly projected in the coming decade is a nation of overwhelming economic power. He also stressed the rising tide of nationalism in Southeast Asia and in the Third World in general. From the picture he has drawn, we see the second largest economic power in an era of rising nationalism having to depend for the security of its vital interests and for the protection of its industrial lifelines on a military power beyond its own control. This picture has absolutely no precedent in history. I think it is an unnatural, anti-historic picture, and I cannot imagine how it can last. The only alternative Ambassador Reischauer can see is a remilitarized Japan, an alternative with enormous disadvantages and likely to be rejected by a large part of the Japanese population. If this is truly the dilemma, I can see nothing but evil prospects. Is there not a third choice, a positive one? Couldn't the United States and Japan use their great political and economic influence during this coming decade to get a sensible reform of the United Nations Security Council and to obtain a collective security system that would avoid both the hegemony and military dominance of either one in this crucial era?

AMBASSADOR REISCHAUER: Let me admit that Japan's unusual situation is an historical paradox. For many reasons the Japanese don't want to, and their neighbors don't want them to, restore themselves as a major military power. In these circumstances, their dependence upon us for their essential security is unnatural unless we can look upon this arrangement as a first small step toward the international solution you have in mind. Perhaps ad-hoc international bodies can begin to build an international control that will eventually extend to a world-wide security system under the United Nations. But I think it will be a long time before a really effective United Nations can provide true security.

I would like to see the American-Japanese military relationship gradually broadened to include other powers like Australia, Canada, and, in the long run, the European nations. I would like to see the Soviet Union join, and eventually even China. But I think the American-Japanese relationship I suggested is a step in that direction and the only possible one at this time.

MR. SHIONOYA: Like Mrs. Borgese, I find disturbing implications in what Ambassador Reischauer has said. More than once he has emphasized the possibility of an outbreak of war in Korea and the vulnerability of the Japanese oil-supply route through the waters around an unstable Indonesia. The implication for the future is that Japan must assume a heavier military burden. I have noted this same kind of thinking among some of my colleagues who praise the Japanese defense force and our ability to improve it, a traditional military approach to the question of Asian stability.

Recently I talked with the leaders of Japan's militant student movements, the rabid *Zengakuren,* and the pro-communist *Yoyogi* group. I wish to emphasize that I do not agree with all their ideas, but I believe we must not forget their significance and the disruptive role these students may play in the debate on renewal of the Japanese-American Security Treaty.

These militants and the more moderate students who belong to neither the *Zengakuren* nor the *Yoyogi* group have been deeply impressed by the military orientation of United States foreign policy in Asia. They have watched the escalation in Vietnam with growing cynicism and concern, giving little or no credence to former President Johnson's protestations of peaceful intent. Official statements by Premier Sato and Mr. Johnson to the effect that Japan must now move ahead on her own, together with the conjectures of Japanese military commentators who predict that America's next moves will be in Korea and the Middle East, have helped to shape student attitudes. The students are suspicious and critical of American militarism in general and of Japanese official collaboration in particular. When the Security Treaty comes up for review, we can expect a great outcry from the students against the maintainance of American bases in Japan.

The danger of anti-American student sentiment is that it can easily be converted into an effort to sever Japanese-American relations and to change the Japanese constitution and rearm the country. The students see the American containment policy not as positive and peaceful but as belligerent —*fujikome*—and American air bases in the Far East as stepping stones to further military action in Asia, particularly against China. Violence within the United States, like the assassinations of the Kennedy brothers, confirms their suspicion that America is committed to a warlike approach.

As long as the students feel that their protests are being

shoved aside, they will remain a dangerous force working against any continuation of the Japanese-American security relationship. Perhaps, as Ambassador Reischauer says, the United States does not apply pressure to influence Japanese foreign policy, but large elements among the Japanese feel coerced. Popular emotion plays an important role in diplomatic relationships.

What we need now, I believe, is not an extension of traditional military thinking but a discussion of the alternatives to present policy that might allay the students' fears and dissipate the sense of crisis so apparent in Japan today.

AMBASSADOR REISCHAUER: I am distressed at the misunderstanding of what I had meant to convey. I have always been against Japan's taking any larger military role than her present limited commitment to defense. I worry that in the coming period of crisis between the United States and Japan a fundamental change in our relationship might lead Japan back to militarism.

It is easy to define what we want in the blissful future, but we are dealing with human nature as it is in 1969 and the messy, unpleasant problems we face today. On the one hand, we have public sentiment in America that Japan must take over the military load in the Far Pacific. On the other hand, we have a multiplicity of Japanese human reactions.

Many Westerners and Japanese have asked me, "Can Japan be a great nation without being also a great military nation, a nuclear nation?" I think Japan can be much greater if she does not go down the road to remilitarization. In the present world where an excess of military power maintains a precarious balance of terror, individual military capacity is no longer significant. Japan can play a much greater, more useful, and more influential role in her part of the world if she becomes the third largest nation while she eschews a big military role.

My great fear is the possible Japanese reaction to America's suddenly moving out of the Far East. Today most Japanese are overwhelmingly against rearmament. But if the Seventh Fleet were withdrawn, and with it all American interest in that part of the world, I can foresee a sudden change in Japanese popular attitudes and an immediate demand for

Japan's remilitarization. To me, keeping the American-Japanese relationship alive is the surest way for Japan to avoid rearmament.

I think Japan truly will be the senior partner in our relationship in the future. I look to Japan for aid in redefining the American military role, a much smaller role than our present one, and in helping us to avoid military misadventures like Vietnam.

AMBASSADOR GOLDBERG: We would be doing a great disservice to our Japanese colleagues if we failed to give them a frank and accurate appraisal of American opinion on the question of reconciling Japan and the United States with China. If the thesis is true that the containment theory is no longer valid and if conferences like this succeed in convincing the American people that China is not the threat they have been told she was, the public will ask, "Why the great military presence in Asia? Why the Defense Treaty? Why the United States and not Japan?"

We have been substantially injured in Southeast Asia. A President of the United States has elected not to run and the overwhelming assumption among the American people is that Mr. Nixon, mindful of the tragic circumstances of President Johnson's political demise, will proceed to wind up the war.

The mood of the American people will dictate a pullback from our widespread world commitments, a significant development for Japanese policymakers. Americans by instinct realize that we are overcommitted, that our resources are heavily taxed, and that we are neglecting our domestic concerns. Increasingly, I expect the people of the United States to question the wisdom of such a large force in Asia, just as they have been questioning it in Europe.

Ambassador Reischauer has emphasized the explosive situation in Korea, but, after nearly twenty years, the world community is beginning to say, "Is all this necessary in South Korea? South Korea is a nation. While fifty thousand Americans patrol that country, fifty thousand South Koreans fight in Vietnam. Couldn't South Korea defend herself with America as an ally instead of the United States being the principal contender?"

Present sentiment for drastically reducing the American presence in Asia does not yet predominate in American opinion, and certainly not in government circles. But as the thesis that China is not a severe threat takes hold, the zeal for heavy American participation in Asia will surely dissipate.

SENATOR COOPER: As Ambassador Goldberg has said, because of the Senate hearings on China policy in 1966 and in response to the urging of scholars, Americans are more and more vigorously questioning the policy of the containment of China. I believe the United States is trying even now to pull away from the land mass of Asia.

How far back will we pull? Have we any interest at all in staying in the far Pacific? Do the Japanese feel that we have no interests there? What course would they recommend?

During this discussion I have felt a strong sentiment among the Japanese for American withdrawal from the mainland of Asia, but I have sensed far less certainty about the wisdom of pulling away from the defense of Japan proper. But even as our Japanese colleagues have affirmed their support for a renewed Security Treaty, I have felt an underlying desire to terminate this arrangement. Do you really want us to leave Japan's defenses to the Japanese? If you believe you can defend yourself, why don't you say so, without reservation? Why don't you arouse your own public opinion? Why don't the Japanese tell us quite frankly, "We don't want your bases; we can defend ourselves. Go!"

As doubt about the wisdom of our containment policy gains momentum in the United States, many people will prefer to see us withdraw entirely from the Far East. Should the Japanese ask that we leave, I believe there would be a positive response from this country.

"We are against no one except the domestic and foreign reactionaries who hinder us from doing business.

"When we have beaten the internal and external reactionaries by uniting all domestic and international forces, we shall be able to do business and establish diplomatic relations with all foreign countries on the basis of equality, mutual respect for territorial integrity and sovereignty."
Mao Tse-tung

---

9   Recognition of Communist China: Points for Consideration

STATEMENTS BY:

Alan Cranston
Edwin O. Reischauer
J.W. Fulbright
Mark O. Hatfield
Don Edwards
Aiichiro Fujiyama

ALAN CRANSTON:

Until the United States establishes diplomatic relations with China, finding solutions to both present and future problems of a specific nature between the two countries is certain to run into difficulty. Recognition need not be sudden nor need it be mutual in the beginning. If the United States were to announce candidly that the American government expects to establish relations whenever mainland China is willing, the burden of improving communications would thereafter fall on Peking, not on Washington.

A vital step leading to American recognition of China would be a reëvaluation of the meaning of the term. From the birth of our nation until the Woodrow Wilson era, recognition did not imply approval, nor non-recognition disapproval, of any nation. American policy for nearly a century and a half based recognition on the *control* a given government could exercise over a populated geographical area. The nature or ideological bias of the government played no part in determining whether or not the United States would recognize its legitimacy.

During the Wilson Administration early in this century, moral judgments entered American decisions on recognition. From that time on the United States has presumably recognized only those countries whose political systems met with official approval, and non-recognition has become an expression of castigation. Inconsistencies have been rampant, and the record shows numerous instances of totalitarian nations enjoying United States recognition despite our moralistic stand.

The time for reversion to our historic attitude on recognition is at hand. The United States Senate might well make a policy declaration, or recommend it to the Executive, that from this day forward recognition will cease to imply approval of what a government stands for.*

---

*On May 27, 1969, Senator Cranston introduced a Senate resolution, co-sponsored by Senator Aiken of Vermont, stating that it was the sense of the Senate that recognition of a regime by the United States should no longer imply approval of that regime.

Such a policy declaration would have an immediate twofold effect: the door would be open for the United States to recognize mainland China and several other governments with ideologies different from our own when it appears in our interest to do so; and those in the United States who advocate recognition of the People's Republic on pragmatic grounds would be cleared automatically of the onus of "communist sympathizer." The American people could be expected to accept an executive or legislative declaration of this kind without severe political reaction.

Only if the way is prepared for eventual diplomatic recognition can the United States begin to proceed along the path of accord in its dealings with the largest nation on the planet.

EDWIN O. REISCHAUER:

Recognition in its larger sense is not a simple problem but a many-sided issue. If we break it into its simplest components, recognition means first of all *de facto* acknowledgement that a given government exists and, secondly, ultimate diplomatic relations.

De facto recognition that China is China presents no real challenge to the American imagination. The United States government still pretends that Taiwan is China, as does the Japanese government, and this legal fiction should be abandoned in favor of the reality that China can be no other than that great historic continental country ruled from Peking today.

Ultimate diplomatic recognition involves two lateral problems: the international status of Taiwan and the related question of Chinese representation in the United Nations. Taiwan is one of the larger political entities in the United Nations today, but, compared to the continent of China, Taiwan is small indeed. Neither of these questions can be ignored, and the solution to both may have to precede ultimate diplomatic recognition.

There are way stations between *de facto* and ultimate recognition, however. Gradual relaxation of tension in fields other than the political can pave the way for eventual diplomatic accommodation. Trade in non-strategic goods, relaxed travel restrictions, cultural exchange, a modification of the United States military posture, and American willingness to discuss peripheral issues would all prepare the ground for eventual diplomatic accord. As for Japan, if the Japanese government were to find a way to recognize Communist China, I believe Japan's relations with the United States would not suffer any setback.

J. W. FULBRIGHT:

It has been officially admitted and seems finally to be generally accepted in the United States that there is nothing that we, much less the Nationalist Chinese on Taiwan, can do to bring about the collapse of the present mainland government. Nevertheless, the hope still seems to persist in certain quarters, both here and abroad, that the Chinese will rise up and overturn their communist rulers. This hope was nurtured by the turmoil in China known as the Great Proletarian Cultural Revolution.

Those who have regarded the Cultural Revolution as evidence of an imminent collapse of China seem to me to have misunderstood this phenomenon. It now seems clear that this strange disruption was really a struggle between the more militant Chinese ideologists, the old revolutionary veterans who wished to keep revolutionary fervor at a high pitch regardless of its consequences, and the more pragmatic managers

137

and scientists who preferred to see ideology subordinated to more practical considerations. The Cultural Revolution did leave certain questions unanswered, questions relating to whether the Chinese revolution would move in new directions or continue in the same general pattern, but they concerned the *course* of the regime's future and had nothing whatsoever to do with the question of whether that regime will *have* a future.

I am not an advocate of immediate, unilateral recognition, for I believe that in the present circumstances such action might have harmful repercussions in other countries. But I do believe that we should declare ourselves ready and willing to reach agreement on the question of recognition whenever the Peking government is willing to do so.

There have been some signs recently that the Chinese may be willing to lift the western fringe of the bamboo curtain at least a little. Specifically, I refer to the Chinese suggestion that the Warsaw talks with the United States be resumed after a lapse of more than a year. Although those talks failed to materialize at the last minute, the language of the Chinese proposal indicated some willingness on their part to adopt a more flexible approach to the United States.

The Chinese announcement suggesting a resumption of talks stated that the Chinese government had consistently adhered to two principles in earlier talks: first that the United States "undertake to withdraw immediately all its armed forces" from Taiwan and the Taiwan Straits "and dismantle all its military installations" in Taiwan; the second, that the United States government "agree that China and the United States conclude an agreement on the five principles of peaceful coexistence."

As far as I am aware, the language used in this statement with regard to Taiwan is more restricted than past public pronouncements devoted to relations with the United States. While it asked for the withdrawal of American armed forces from Taiwan and the dismantling of American military installations there, it made no specific reference to any Chinese determination to liberate Taiwan, an omission noted by the Soviets who might be expected to be particularly sensitive to every nuance. While this omission does not mean that the

Chinese have changed their attitude on the question of Taiwan's future, it does give us an encouraging sign.

The language regarding agreement on the principles of peaceful coexistence was another such indication. The Chinese have made no reference to peaceful coexistence with the United States since the mid-nineteen-fifties, to the best of my knowledge. I am intrigued by the fact that the Chinese were suddenly moved to state publicly that they were willing to agree with the United States on "the five principles of peaceful coexistence." These principles are propositions on which we *should* be able to agree: respect for each other's sovereignty and territorial integrity; abstention from aggression and threats against each other; abstention from interference or intervention in the internal affairs of one another; recognition of the equality of races; and recognition of the equality of all nations, large and small. I do not see how this list can be improved upon as a general prescription for future relations between any two states.

The balance of power may be an old principle, but it is certainly not obsolete. Perhaps if we act wisely, it will assume a new and more constructive importance that will bring unsuspected and unanticipated benefits not only to us but to many nations and will improve the prospects for peace in the Pacific. History is replete with far more curious paradoxes.

MARK O. HATFIELD:

Americans tend to believe that recognition is a prerequisite to all relationships with China. On the contrary, we can establish economic, cultural, and other relations, as Australia, Canada, and Japan have done, without necessarily confronting the political recognition issue. Public misunderstanding, as Senator Cranston has said, has led Americans to suspend all activities with respect to China pending the resolution of the political questions involved in formal recognition.

The United States should pursue every opportunity to encourage contact between Americans and Chinese at both governmental and private levels. As a matter of the highest priority, the United States should assure that Peking is at least invited to attend international meetings on disarmament. Including China on the invitation list will not insure that she will attend nor will it guarantee that her participation will be constructive. But agreements on disarmament and nuclear non-proliferation will be no more than futile diplomatic exercises if they are not signed by Peking.

One American policy, that of deliberately precluding Chinese participation in important non-strategic international conferences, does our government no credit. Approximately five thousand such conferences take place each year and, among government-sponsored meetings, more than half involve the participation of communist nations. Mainland China attends very few of these meetings, partly because Communist China refuses to sit down at a conference table with the Nationalists. A State Department official confessed to me that the United States deliberately exploits Peking's attitude. "We have taken pains to see that the Nationalist Chinese attend these meetings to forestall Chinese Communist participation," he told me, explaining that the United States makes sure that Taiwan's dues are paid and that Taiwan's representatives have transportation to the conference site.

Our persistent attempts to exclude China from the community of nations have tended to confirm Peking's view of the United States as a hostile, unyielding enemy and, in addition, have contained a built-in boomerang. Our allies, whom we have tried to persuade to join us in denying recognition to Peking, have resisted our arm-twisting as they have discovered the cost of isolating China. One by one, they have established some form of contact with the continent. As a result the United States has isolated itself from the more moderate attitudes and policies of its friends.

DON EDWARDS:

Political leadership can greatly influence public attitudes. In the early thirties, shortly after Franklin Delano Roosevelt was elected President, the United States faced an impasse with the Soviet Union similar to our present difficulty with Communist China. After careful negotiation with the U.S.S.R., President Roosevelt announced a resumption of diplomatic relations with the Soviet Union, together with rosy plans for trade expansion between the two countries. Following an initial reaction of shock, the country accepted the government's decision without undue alarm.

I believe that the White House has similar leeway today to negotiate with the People's Republic of China toward recognition. I do not believe that such action by the President would have any traumatic effect on the American people. Firm, enlightened policymakers have always had the capacity to mold public opinion.

AIICHIRO FUJIYAMA:

Most Japanese believe that recognition of mainland China should be achieved step by step, and most agree that the difficult question of Taiwan is a domestic issue to be solved by the Chinese themselves. But while the world is waiting for the Chinese to reach a solution, Japan can continue her efforts to improve relations.

Today we have private trade and fishing agreements with China. Perhaps if Peking's commercial representatives were

141

allowed to establish offices in Japan and their Japanese counterparts opened offices in Peking, these private trade and fishing agreements could gradually take on an official character. The present attitude of the Japanese government is all too negative.

As Senator Cranston has pointed out, the historic American concept of recognition has changed during this century, and, regrettably, Japan has adopted a concept identical with the present United States interpretation. In the early postwar days the Japanese harbored a great fear of communism. This fear took deep root in the minds of the people, and it influenced Japanese policy.

Interestingly enough, Japanese history has a parallel to President Roosevelt's action in recognizing the Soviet Union. When Ichiro Hatoyama was Prime Minister, he recognized Soviet Russia in the face of strong opposition from within the party itself. The irony is that those who opposed recognition at that time, especially Japanese businessmen, today express their contentment with Japanese-Soviet relations; they have a keen interest in U.S.S.R.-Japan trade and joint Soviet-Japanese economic development. As politicians, we in the Japanese Diet feel that we have an obligation to lead public opinion toward accepting a change in Japan's concept of the meaning of recognition so that official China policy may be similar to Japan's present policy toward the Soviet Union.

"There is no such thing as a 'pro-foreign' Chinese. . . .
"What is probably not comprehensible from abroad is
the extent to which even anti-communist Chinese
support Peking on any nationalistic issue."
Edgar Snow

10   Taiwan

THE PITFALLS AND CONTRADICTIONS IN JAPAN'S TAIWAN-CHINA POLICIES

A STATEMENT BY
Tokuma Utsunomiya

THE TWO FACES OF FORMOSA: MODEL OF PROGRESS AND SYMBOL OF STAGNATION

A STATEMENT BY
William O. Douglas

THE PITFALLS AND CONTRADICTIONS
IN JAPAN'S TAIWAN-CHINA POLICIES

TOKUMA UTSUNOMIYA:

The Japanese approach to the problem
of Taiwan is governed by conflicting, inconsistent attitudes
toward the Chiang Kai-shek regime, by economic considerations, and by natural Japanese sympathy for the aspiration of
the Taiwanese islanders to self-determination. Popular sentiment is fluid at present, but a growing number of Japanese,
particularly those of the younger generations, are beginning to
doubt the wisdom of Japan's official Taiwan policy and to
protest the strained relations with mainland China that it
generates.

Taiwan became a Japanese territory as a result of the
Sino-Japanese war in 1894-1895. For roughly half a century,
until Japan's defeat in the Second World War, Taiwan was
under Japanese rule. This period coincided with a time of
confusion and chaos in China. Wars, civil strife, and colonialism served to intensify China's backwardness, but Taiwan
by contrast enjoyed relative social stability and economic
well-being. Improved methods of cultivating rice and sugar-
cane were devised, and the island achieved a certain degree
of industrialization. Taiwan escaped destruction in the Second
World War, and at the war's end the Taiwanese enjoyed better
living conditions than the people of devastated Japan.

When the Chinese Nationalists landed on the island in the
wake of the Chinese civil war, the Taiwanese, with consider-

able justification, regarded Chiang's troops as morally and socially inferior and Chiang Kai-shek's government as authoritarian and corrupt. The ten million islanders, who are mostly of Chinese origin, outnumbered the newly arrived "outside provincials" loyal to Chiang Kai-shek by a ratio of 5-1. Near the end of 1947 the "Two-Two-Eight Incident" occurred; riots started in Taipei and spread throughout the entire island. Chinese reinforcements hastily dispatched from the continent crushed the rebellion, but the Taiwanese still harbor a deep distrust of the Nationalist Chinese. Today Chiang Kai-shek's authoritarian rule depends on the vigilance of a police force of six hundred thousand men backed by an army of equal size.

Japanese who visit Taiwan today remark on the nostalgic attitude of many Taiwanese toward Japan. While the islanders do speak Japanese and are steeped in Japanese culture, Japan would be making a great mistake to interpret these signs as a desire on the part of Taiwan to become a Japanese colony once again.

The question of self-determination for Taiwan must not be considered with nostalgia or sentimentality. If the people of Taiwan truly desire self-determination and independence, they must face its serious implications. Self-determination would amount to an immediate act of revolt against the police state of Chiang Kai-shek and a long-range revolution against all governments of China. The Japanese cannot recognize the government of Chiang Kai-shek on the one hand and support self-determination for the Taiwanese on the other. If Japan were to give serious thought to supporting self-determination for Taiwan, she would need to come up with concrete, impartial proposals regarding the time, method, and procedures.

True self-determination would be, at best, difficult to achieve. Chiang's government has been able to maintain not only its position of prestige in the United Nations and other international bodies but also its right to rule Taiwan as the legitimate government of China. If the Chiang Kai-shek regime were not supported by the United States, it would be no more than a government in exile. With American support, however, Chiang maintains his seat of power in Taipei while the government of the province of Taiwan has been removed to Taichung. Furthermore, of the 773 seats in the Legislative Yuan in Taipei, only 464 are held by members who actually live on Taiwan and only fourteen represent Taiwan itself. Chiang Kai-shek maintains the fiction that the Legislative Yuan in Taipei represents the whole of China, and the remaining seats are reserved for "Chinese." Were the Taiwanese to establish home rule by plebiscite, Nationalist Chinese authority would be restricted to Quemoy and Matsu Islands. Furthermore, 457 of the representatives in the Yuan would also have to move to Quemoy and Matsu.

The Peking government frequently reiterates that it will, without fail, liberate Taiwan, but "liberation" does not mean self-determination. Like Chiang Kai-shek, Peking's interest is in achieving unification of all China. The Communists firmly reject the principle of two Chinas and will oppose any legal separation of Taiwan from China, including the creation of an independent state of Taiwan. In Peking I have heard the expression, "Chiang Kai-shek Hsien-sheng (teacher) is our comrade." In a perverse sense, Chiang *is* the comrade of the mainland Chinese. Should his claim to sovereign power over "one" China collapse, the People's Republic would lose a powerful supporter of her own assertion that the government of China may legally exercise hegemony over all historically Chinese territory. It is significant that China bombards Quemoy and Matsu periodically but makes no serious attempt to take over the islands and destroy Chiang Kai-shek Hsiensheng.

Japanese official policy toward Taiwan and the mainland is both complex and ill-advised, and Japan cannot continue for long on her present course. The total volume of trade between mainland China and Japan now exceeds five hundred million dollars a year, even in the face of adverse political conditions. The western waters of the China Sea, close to the Chinese coastline, are important Japanese commercial fishing grounds. Annual private agreements with Peking have insured the safety of fishermen in these waters, but diplomatic affairs have reached a stage where private negotiations are becoming difficult, if not impossible. If frozen diplomatic relations between Japan and Communist China continue, not only will Japanese commercial interests be at stake but the fate of her citizens and the disposal of her war dead on the continent will remain unresolved. Japan's lack of diplomatic relations with China can be characterized, therefore, only as an act of sabotage by the Japanese government against the people of Japan.

The Taiwan government insists on this act of sabotage from Japan and demands that the Japanese people give up the natural benefits arising from commercial relations with mainland China. The promise extracted from the Japanese government and embodied in the so-called Yoshida Letter, named after the late Prime Minister Shigeru Yoshida, is that Japan will not permit use of funds from the Export-Import Bank to finance the export of factories to continental China on a deferred payment basis. Taiwan is, of course, free to claim that it is the legitimate government of China but has no right to use this claim to prevent the improvement of relations between Japan and continental China.

Technically Japan is still at war with mainland China. The Japanese-Nationalist China peace treaty, signed in 1952 during the John Foster Dulles era, does not apply to the mainland. Ironically, the treaty brought peace between Japan and a part of China—Taiwan—with which she was never at war, but it left Japan at war with the seven hundred million people on the continent. This treaty is and has been a source of insecurity and instability in the Far East.

Meanwhile, Japan has been strengthening her ties with Taiwan. One factor promoting the relationship is the respect some Japanese accord to Chiang Kai-shek as an anti-communist hero, but more important is Japan's favorable balance of trade with Taiwan.

Japan's exports to Taiwan, which averaged $60 millions between 1954 and 1958, have risen sharply to $210 millions in 1965, $250 millions in 1966, and $320 millions in 1967. By contrast, imports from Taiwan, which averaged around $60 millions between 1954 and 1958, have increased only to between $130 and $150 millions in the last few years. The sharp increases in exports were chiefly in machinery, steel, and textiles, all products connected in one way or another with the war in Vietnam. At the same time these exports have been financed mostly by Japanese loans and investments in Taiwan's industry. Japan's main imports from Taiwan used to be rice and sugar. Today bananas and lumber have replaced them, and Taiwan's exports to Japan have reached their limit.

From Taiwan's point of view, the basic problem of her economy lies in her chronic unfavorable trade balance. Taiwan's trade deficit has been covered by U.S. economic aid, which has run close to a billion dollars a year, and by procurements for the U.S. forces stationed both there and in Vietnam. But the war in Vietnam must some day come to an end, and, since 1965, American economic aid to Taiwan has been cut off except for surplus agricultural products.

Taiwan has been concentrating since 1967 on inducing foreign capital into the country as a countermeasure and has achieved a certain degree of success. Her basic weaknesses are heavy governmental spending on armaments and rigid markets. The military dictatorship spends sixty per cent of the total budget for military purposes, and Japan and the United States account for forty-five per cent of her imports and sixty to seventy per cent of her exports. Since Taiwan cannot rely forever on the United States, she must reduce armaments and concentrate on internal administration and economy. The best way for Taiwan to stimulate her economy would be for her to negotiate the opening of trade with the continent of China.

China's attitudes, of course, will determine future Sino-Japanese relations as much as Japan's or Taiwan's aspirations will. What is the Chinese position on better relations with Japan? Is Taiwan an insurmountable barrier to a rapprochement between the two countries? I gained some valuable insights from Prime Minister Chou En-lai and Foreign Minister Chen-yi when I visited the mainland in 1961 and again in 1967. On the first occasion Chou outlined a practical approach to an improvement in Sino-Japanese relations:

We desire from our hearts friendship with Japan.

For the sake of friendship between our two countries, let us seek out and count the points of agreement instead of emphasizing the points of disagreement.

We are agreed on our opposition to the revival of militarism in the Far East.

We are agreed that the Taiwan question is an internal problem and that Taiwan belongs to a unified China.

We are agreed that although Japan and China differ in their social and political structures, both countries should mutually tolerate these differences and that peaceful coexistence is possible and necessary.

We are agreed in our support of the Ishibashi proposal for the creation of a Far East peace maintenance structure, participated in by Japan, China, the United States, and the Soviet Union, based on the condition that the United States first withdraw its offensive military might from the vicinity of Taiwan.

Chou En-Lai's fourth point assumed the possibility of a reconciliation between the United States and China, depending on the attitude and initiative of Japan, and of a regional security structure in the Far East.

In 1967 Foreign Minister Chen-yi elaborated on the Chinese approach to foreign affairs:

We will support national liberation movements in Asia, Africa, and Latin America. We will promote peaceful coexistence with countries having differing social systems from ours. We will not aggress against any country or intervene in its internal affairs. We will strengthen our ties with socialist countries. In the case of the Soviet Union, it broke off its ties with us.

The present situation involving the United States, China, and Taiwan could have had a precedent in Europe after the Bolshevik revolution. Immediately after the October Revolution in Russia, General Anton Ivanovich Denikin and General Piotr Nikolayevich Wrangel established an anti-revolutionary regime in southwestern Russia. If Great Britain had protected this regime by a military force on the Crimean Peninsula and recognized it as the legitimate government of all Russia, she would have created an impasse similar to the present one in the Far East and prevented the eventual improvement of relations between London and Moscow.

If we were to eliminate the military problems that have arisen from United States endorsement of Chiang's regime as the legitimate government of China, almost nothing would hinder an understanding between Washington and Peking. In the words of Chen-yi once more, "Once the Taiwan problem is settled, United States-China relations would practically all be solved."

A resolution of the Taiwan problem, it seems to me, would demand four initial steps. First, the withdrawal from Taiwan of the United States military bases that Peking regards as takeoff points for armed reconnaissance flights over the mainland. Second, a limitation on the range of activity of United States air and naval forces in the vicinity of the China Sea, including the Taiwan Straits. Third, the withdrawal from Okinawa of American nuclear weapons, which are aimed at various cities on mainland China. And finally, the use of United States influence to effect the withdrawal of major Nationalist forces and heavy weapons from Quemoy and Matsu, including commando troops maintained to infiltrate the mainland, and the reduction of all forces there to the level of garrison troops.

The Peking government cannot be expected to abandon its claim that Taiwan is under the sovereignty of China, but the evidence is that Peking would not embark on any hasty attempts to unify Taiwan by force, particularly if Taipei and Peking have the prospects of a mutually beneficial economic exchange. If Taiwan, like Hong Kong, seems capable of little harm but of much benefit to the People's Republic, Peking would be unlikely to seek a change in the status quo through the use of force. The Chinese are noted for their pragmatism, and Peking's record with regard to Hong Kong and Macao indicates that when Taiwan no longer seems a base for attack against the mainland, the island's theoretical status will cause little trouble. For the present, a more permanent resolution of the Taiwan problem must be left to the placid flow of time.

THE TWO FACES OF FORMOSA:
MODEL OF PROGRESS
AND SYMBOL OF STAGNATION

WILLIAM O. DOUGLAS:

The starting point for the initiation of a coöperative regime of law, diplomacy, and friendly intercourse with Peking is the resolution of the Formosa problem. At the legal level there are a wide variety of views, and each is colored by the political approach one takes to the Peking-Taipei issue.

In the British view, Formosa remained Japanese territory until the peace treaty was signed at San Francisco and became effective April 28, 1952. The interim management of the island by the Chinese Nationalists from 1945 to 1952 did not create a right of legal sovereignty. To the British, the Chinese Nationalists do not represent China; and Formosa does not "belong" to Peking because that government has no effective control over the territory. Since the San Francisco Treaty did not assign Formosa to any power, the British maintain that its status remains to be settled by multilateral international agreement.

The United States recognizes the Nationalist regime on Formosa as the government of China. How America can justify this position remains a mystery since the Nationalists command no sovereignty over a single acre of the vast mainland. Apart from that, the British and United States viewpoints coalesce in concluding that neither the surrender of Japanese forces on Formosa to the Nationalists nor the San Francisco Treaty, nor any prior act, constituted formal transfer of the island to any China group. The problem remains—in the United States view—a problem for multilateral international settlement, preferably by the United Nations.

Peking and Taipei approach the problem differently. They maintain that when Japan surrendered, Formosa became an integral unit of the territory of China. Both insist that when China repudiated the 1895 treaty ceding Formosa to Japan, Formosa reverted to China. Both denounce the idea that there may be two Chinas and that the United Nations has any function to perform in resolving the status of Formosa.

As a political problem touching seven hundred million Chinese, the legal conclusion of both Peking and Taipei that Formosa "belongs" to China must for all practical purposes be the starting point for seeking a solution. The creation of two Chinas is not politically feasible. The maintenance of Formosa as an armed camp keeps Asia inflamed and is a constant source of irritation, turmoil, and hatred. Placing Formosa under some form of trusteeship, until present attitudes mellow and the fresh approaches of a new generation germinate, seems the only practical course.

Doubtless there are Japanese who have changed very little, merely dropping their old anti-communist, pro-Nazi flag for a new anti-communist, pro-American flag. Yet Japan, as I understand her, is a medley of voices, and many Japanese recognize that the key to Asia's future is a birth of friendship among Japan, Peking, and the United States.

The mainland's quarrel with Formosa need not be either Japan's quarrel or America's. Throughout history outside nations have become divisive influences in China by recognizing regional governments who were only local warlords opposed to Peking. Both the United States and Japan serve that role again in recognizing Taipei.

We of the West embrace the Nationalists as if they were the symbols of democracy as opposed to communism and of free enterprise as opposed to socialism. Yet, if civil rights are one measure of democracy, Formosa sets a totalitarian example.

In style, Chiang Kai-shek's campaigns against the intellectuals closely resemble Peking's campaign against those who fail to conform to communist orthodoxy. Lei Chen's conviction in 1960 and his subsequent sentence of ten years because of his efforts to form the China Democratic Party as an anti-communist opposition party in Formosa are well-known. Not so well-known is the recent military trial of seven men who promoted reforms but went no further than to discuss "radical ideas," a common procedure at any American university worth its salt. Pressure for intellectual conformity is so strong in Formosa that no more than five per cent of the students who go abroad to study return. Taipei can talk about economic "progress," but when it comes to matters of the intellect, in both the humanities and politics, Formosa is a symbol of stagnation.

Free enterprise versus socialism has never been an issue on the mainland. The issues there have been vast corruption and hopeless inefficiency. In terms of capitalism, Taiwan is modern in one sense and exploitative in another. The drive for industrialization continues with plants for wire, electronic equipment, umbrellas, jewelry, steel, and shipbuilding going up under an ambitious master plan. But Formosa's secret and abundant resource is low-cost labor, which capital gladly exploits. When that labor supply becomes more sophisticated and demands higher wages, Formosan labor will become less attractive, and unexploited Korea will supply the new low-cost labor for exploitative capitalism. Much good work is done on Formosa, especially in the agricultural sector, but the island is not a symbol of virtuous capitalism seeking to survive in an evil socialist sea. Moreover, Formosa's military establishment consumes eleven per cent of her gross national product, the highest percentage expenditure in the world, and this figure takes no account of the vast funds that pour in from the United States for defense.

The great issue that sweeps both the mainland and Formosa is nationalism, and the United States has no rightful concern with that issue. A China unified under Peking's control need pose no more of a threat either to America's or to Japan's vital interests than a Peking without command over Formosa.

". . . to practice tolerance and live together in peace with one another as good neighbors, and
"to unite our strength to maintain international peace and security, and
"to ensure, by the acceptance of principles and the institution of methods, that armed force shall not be used, save in the common interest, and
"to employ international machinery for the promotion of the economic and social advancement of all peoples . . . ."
Preamble to the United Nations Charter

---

11   Chinese Representation in the United Nations

COMMUNIST CHINESE MEMBERSHIP: A FIRST STEP TOWARD WORLD PEACE

A STATEMENT BY
Aiichiro Fujiyama

A TWO-CHINA POLICY FOR THE UNITED STATES

A STATEMENT BY
Arthur Goldberg

THE VALUE OF
A UNITED STATES INITIATIVE

A STATEMENT BY
Edward M. Kennedy

A POSSIBLE ROLE
FOR THE UNITED NATIONS

A STATEMENT BY
Elisabeth Mann Borgese

COMMENTS BY:

Alan Cranston
Edwin O. Reischauer
Chester A. Ronning
Harvey Wheeler

COMMUNIST CHINESE MEMBERSHIP:
A FIRST STEP TOWARD WORLD PEACE

AIICHIRO FUJIYAMA:

If peace and stability are ever to be achieved in Asia, the People's Republic of China must enter the international comity of nations. The initial step in ending her isolation would be to invite her, as one of the world's largest powers, to take a seat in the United Nations, where she may meet and talk with representatives of other countries.

Probably the greatest barrier to Chinese participation in international discussions and coöperative world-wide enterprises has been the attitude of the United States toward seating the Peking government in the United Nations, either as the representative of China or as one of the successor states. From the onset of the Korean War to the present, the United States has, both by positive action and negative response, rejected mainland China's right to join the United Nations. As a major power in the Security Council, the United States has used its prestige to defeat all attempts to give membership to Peking.

In 1950 the United Nations General Assembly adopted a resolution branding the People's Republic of China as an aggressor in Korea. From 1951 to 1960 each successive General Assembly passed a draft resolution "not to consider the question of the representation of China." This was the period of the so-called moratorium formula.

After 1960 the General Assembly entered a period of repeated confrontation between the Albanian Resolution and the Important Question Resolution. The Albanian Resolution, defeated each time, was aimed at expelling the Nationalist Republic of China and installing the Communist People's

Republic in her place. The favored Important Question Resolution stated that "any proposal to change the representation of China is an important question," to be decided only by a two-thirds majority vote.

Opposition to Communist Chinese membership reached its lowest level in 1965 when the Important Question Resolution won approval by only seven votes, while the ballots cast for and against the Albanian Resolution were equal. Since then the Important Question Resolution has gained favor slightly, a reflection of such developments as the failure of Chinese diplomacy in Africa, the Sino-Soviet split, and Peking's general confusion on international issues.

I feel that revision of the United Nations Charter is urgently needed. In Asia we have three divided countries, compared to one divided country in Europe. In terms of population, a large segment of the human race is involved in these three divided Asian countries, all of which are poor. Poverty compounds the many other problems that the nations of Asia face and is a significant issue for the United Nations to consider. Therefore I believe that two Asian countries should be permanently represented on the Security Council. If Japan does play a larger role on the international scene in the future, as Ambassador Reischauer predicts, I believe Japan should have a permanent seat on the Security Council. At the very least, the United Nations should increase the number of non-permanent Asian seats if two permanent Security Council seats cannot be allocated to Asia. The United Nations was established to insure peace, but conditions have changed tremendously since the early postwar days, and today the United Nations has over 120 independent member countries.

The People's Republic of China shows no will at present to join the United Nations even if she were invited. Regardless of Peking's apparent hostility, an organization established on the principle of universality should keep the door open at all times. The United Nations should substitute for the Important Question Resolution a statement that "the representation of the People's Republic of China in the United Nations is welcome." Such a declaration by the General Assembly would automatically cancel the 1950 "aggressor" resolution and pave the way for an eventual settlement.

Affirming that the People's Republic of China would be welcome in the United Nations would not resolve the difficult question of Chinese representation on the Security Council and the status of the Nationalist government on Taiwan. It would seem, however, that as the *de jure* government of the entire mainland, Peking should be entitled to the permanent Security Council seat. Practically speaking, these difficult problems can be settled on the basis of the responses the respective Chinese regimes choose to make and by an enlargement or reorganization of the Security Council itself.

If specialized United Nations agencies like UNESCO, WHO, and FAO were to issue simultaneous resolutions inviting Peking's participation, the way would be open for mainland China to rejoin international society and thus contribute to easing world tension.

A TWO-CHINA POLICY
FOR THE UNITED STATES

ARTHUR GOLDBERG:

America has no choice but to remain a world power but is under no compulsion to be a world policeman. President Kennedy put his finger on this point when he said: "The United States is neither omnipotent nor omniscient. . . . We cannot impose our will. . . . We cannot right every wrong or reverse each adversity. . . . There cannot be an American solution for every problem."

I believe profoundly that nations, including our own, will never know real security until they acknowledge some impartial and effective international agency designed to keep the peace, control armaments, negotiate settlements, advance human rights, and facilitate social and economic progress. To this end, we should give our help and encouragement to those Asian nations that show the will and the capacity not only to remain independent but also to take an ever-increasing share of responsibility for the security, stability, and growth of the region.

But in a world where survival is still an open question, we have no choice but to persist in the United Nations effort to organize an international order and security that will extend the benefits and restraints of the rule of law to all peoples and all governments. It is high time, therefore, for the United States to support a two-China policy in the United Nations. Our policy should be based on the premise that both the Nationalists and the Communists should sit in the U.N. General Assembly as successors to the China that signed the U.N. Charter. I believe also that the United States should support a change that would permit mainland China to sit on the Security Council.

The groundwork for this move has already been prepared. With the authority of our government, I advanced three propositions for a new American policy on China in the September, 1966, U.N. general debate:

. . . It is not the policy of the United States to isolate Communist China from the world. . . .
. . . The United States will vigorously oppose any effort to exclude the representatives of the Republic of China from the United Nations. . . .
. . . The United States has the friendliest historic feelings toward the great Chinese people and looks forward to the occasion when they will once again enrich, rather than endanger, the fabric of the world community, and, in the spirit of the Charter, "practice tolerance and live together in peace with one another as good neighbors."

Last September I proposed that our United Nations representative be authorized to state at the very outset of the debate in the General Assembly session that "the United States will not oppose admission of representatives of Peking to this Assembly, provided that continued representation of the Republic of China in this Assembly and in the United Nations is assured." I believe the course of action I have proposed has real merit from the viewpoint of both the United States and the Republic of China.

Both major American political parties and their candidates have emphasized the need for ending the isolation of Communist China. Public opinion polls show that the American people are ready for concrete action to give substance to these words. A distinguished panel of experts under the auspices of the United Nations Association has endorsed a two-China policy as a wise and necessary course for our country.

I recognize that this policy would cause difficulties for Taiwan and for some of our allies in Southeast Asia. But there would be far greater difficulties for them and for us if Taiwan were to be expelled from the United Nations, as the Albanian Resolution proposes, and mainland China admitted as the sole successor to China's seat. We should stand steadfast against any effort by Peking and her friends to expel Taiwan from the United Nations. We should also continue to insist that the Republic of China retain the Chinese seat in the Security Council until Peking accepts a two-China policy.

A flexible American attitude would go a long way toward preventing the expulsion of Taiwan from the Assembly. At the same time, it would reinforce our argument that the Security Council should not consider the question of Chinese representation until the Assembly acts and Peking responds. It would be highly unfortunate for the Security Council to take up the question before the two-China formula can be debated in the Assembly, where Taiwan enjoys much greater support. At present the composition of the Security Council is weighted heavily against Taiwan. In contrast, the last vote on Chinese representation in the Assembly was favorable to Taiwan—a great improvement on the 1965 tie vote on the one-China proposal that sought to expel Taiwan from the Assembly.

United States support for a two-China policy in the United Nations should not be interpreted as an American effort to abandon its defense and security commitments to Taiwan. Nor should there be any change in the continuity of our other defense and security arrangements in Asia. If our new China policy, on the other hand, were to provide an incentive to our Asian friends to go ahead with regional arrangements for their own security, it would be advantageous both to them and to the United States.

Peking says it will "never" accept the right of Taiwan to United Nations membership. Under Peking's present intransigent leadership, we can assume it will castigate a two-China proposal. But Mao Tse-tung and his fellow Stalinists are aging. A new leadership generation may react differently. Our new policy would make clear to the world community that Peking and not Washington is keeping mainland China out of the United Nations.

The absence of Peking and its ally, North Vietnam, from the United Nations has been a substantial factor in freezing the world organization out of any peacemaking role in the Vietnam War. Furthermore, Communist China now rejects both the nuclear test-ban treaty and the nuclear non-proliferation treaty. Her professed reason for rejection of the latter is the involvement of the United Nations from which she is excluded. At the least, we should remove the basis for this contention by inviting Peking to U.N. membership; the United Nations is resilient enough to accommodate this unruly new member. At the best, we can look forward to the day when, under new leadership, Communist China "as a recognized member of the world community and the world's fifth atomic power" is ready to join disarmament agreements so essential to world survival.

Peking has condemned the Soviet invasion of Czechoslovakia as a "shameless act" comparable to the Nazi invasion of the Sudetenland. But Communist China herself has been left free to pursue policies of international subversion, immune from even the limited restraints that membership and participation in the United Nations imposes. Through U.N. membership, the Chinese Communists would be given the chance to apply the principle of nonintervention to their own conduct. Given the present conditions in the People's Republic of China, a lessening of tension cannot be achieved solely by our action in support of a two-China policy. But the eventual conciliation we all desire cannot be achieved without such an action on our part.

THE VALUE OF A
UNITED STATES INITIATIVE

EDWARD M. KENNEDY:

I believe that a durable peace in Asia, and the conditions needed to build and maintain viable societies and economies throughout the area, will not emerge unless the United States makes an effort to confront the problem of Sino-American relations with candor. The time is overdue for the government and the people of the United States to engage in a discussion and to reassess our general policy goals in Asia and our China policy in particular. Nothing has happened recently to alter my long-standing view that the United States must take creative initiatives in an effort to break down the great wall of estrangement that now exists between the two countries.

Undoubtedly the most important element in building stable relations between Washington and Peking is to find solutions to the problems of Taiwan and Chinese representation in the United Nations. We can fervently hope that the wedge between Taiwan and the mainland will narrow and a general relaxation of tension in the western Pacific will take place as a consequence. We can even hope that the parties directly involved will examine the possibilities and work toward achieving a better relationship. At the same time I believe that a United States initiative within the United Nations would contribute to a new beginning for our Asia policy.

Before we take any action toward bringing Communist China into the United Nations, we should make unmistakably clear that we will not abrogate our commitments to our friends on Taiwan and that we will work to preserve Taiwan's presence and voice in the United Nations. My strong belief is that Taiwan's case for retention of United Nations membership, if mainland China is finally admitted, would find more support within the international community if the Nationalist Chinese government in Taipei were to bring the ten million native Taiwanese into the mainstream of the island's political life. The United States stands for free institutions in South Vietnam, in all of Asia, and throughout the world. Free institutions should be encouraged in Taiwan as well.

The United States and those who share our objectives would be well-advised to draft and support a resolution at the next session of the United Nations General Assembly recommending the membership of mainland China in the international body. In addition, the United States should work within the United Nations to assure the continued representation of Taiwan.

Allocating the permanent seat on the Security Council held by Taiwan since the founding of the United Nations is a complex problem not easily solved. A number of alternative solutions have been suggested by those expert in these matters. Some have proposed that neither Peking nor Taipei be seated permanently at this time and that the Charter should be revised to reduce the number of seats from five to four. Others have argued that the five permanent seats should be retained, with the fifth seat going to one of the major underdeveloped nations of the world, such as India. It is my view that we should withdraw our opposition to Peking's entry into the United Nations as the representative of China not only in the General Assembly but in the Security Council as well. The seat on the Security Council was granted to China in 1945 in recognition of a great people who had borne a major share of the burden of the Second World War, thereby making the United Nations possible. The seat was not a reward for the particular political group leading the country at the time.

I do not believe that a United States effort along these lines would necessarily produce results, nor do I believe that progress on the issue of China's representation within the United Nations is immediately crucial to a betterment of Sino-American relations. A United States initiative would, however, contribute to American stature in the eyes of our Asian friends and allies. When they observe that America's policy is constructive and flexible enough to encompass their own needs and aspirations, we shall be well on the way toward the basic task of assisting in the development of a stable Asia. The nations of Asia must be the first to live with the China of the future, and all of America's recent Presidents have rightfully committed the United States to help them in their effort to accommodate themselves. We must now move to meet the challenge of China, not on the battlefield but at the conference tables and in the international forums created for peace.

Let the United States give new perspective to its goals in Asia and its policy toward China. All nations must realize that substantive progress toward stability and normal relations between the United States and China will depend, in the end, on China's willingness to renounce force as a means of international change, to negotiate and accept compromises, and to give up her aim of destroying the United States. In the meantime, whatever effort we make to improve our relations with China will serve the deepest traditions of the United States and the highest aspirations of the world. It takes two sides to make a lasting peace but only one to take the first step.

ELISABETH MANN BORGESE:

The relationship of economic aid to coöperation and that of political influence to military security are issues of a general nature in world relations, both present and historical.

Bilateral economic relations may well be kept free from political implications if the two partners are on approximately the same level of economic development. The recent agreement between France and the Soviet Union for joint foreign-trade planning implies neither that France must go communist nor that the Soviet Union must become capitalist. A similar depoliticized relationship could exist today between the United States and Japan, as it obviously could not have existed during the years of occupation and reconstruction following the Second World War.

When there is a heavy economic and political imbalance between the two partners, economic coöperation based on aid inevitably will have political strings attached. The American economic buildup of West Germany, Japan, or Taiwan would have been unthinkable without the establishment of conservative, Western-oriented regimes. That an economic-political system of this kind is dependent, in turn, on a military defense system dominated by the stronger partner seems equally inevitable. That it is impossible—or at least thus far has been impossible—to transfer the control of such a military-political-economic system to the other partner or partners has been demonstrated by the NATO experience.

The maintenance of security systems of the NATO or

SEATO type can insure peace and development for only a limited time and to a limited extent. The moment is bound to come when the burden of an overgrown military apparatus becomes crippling for the economy; the rise of interregional tensions can blow up the system or a decline of such tension can throw it into obsolescence.

The dilemma would be without issue if the only alternative to military-political-economic systems like NATO and SEATO were, as it is often argued in the United States, "abdication of our responsibilities as a great power," the abolition of the security arrangements, abandonment of the political bases, and renunciation of economic aid. But another solution can be found in greater reliance on the United Nations, in the channeling of economic aid and the formulation of development plans through U.N. agencies and organizations. Only after a more equitable economic balance among the various areas of the world has been established through regional coöperation and the United Nations will bilateral American relations become practical, mutually profitable, and free from political and strategic implications. A more effective use of the United Nations would include not only a new emphasis on economic coöperation but also a transfer of security arrangements.

A beginning in this direction could be made by replacing American troops in Vietnam with a U.N. force for the period of transition. Why not consider a similar arrangement on Taiwan until the people of Taiwan, freed from the political, legal, and economic entanglements engendered by the American presence, are in a position freely to determine their own future? Why not make similar shifts to a United Nations presence on Okinawa and on all other "foreign bases" in areas that, under proposals with which the Soviets are in accord, should be de-nuclearized?

An enhanced role for the United Nations must be based on two premises: an improvement of its machinery *by* and *for* such expanded use, that is to say, functional and constitutional changes; and a normalization of the position of the People's Republic of China. Both premises are inextricably connected with and essential to a new approach to the East Asian situation. If placing Taiwan under U.N. trusteeship and recognizing the People's Republic of China should open the way for active Chinese participation in the United Nations, the woefully obsolete structure of the Security Council would need improvement. Without doubt the number of permanent or veto-holding powers must be enlarged. It has been suggested that China's permanent place be turned over to India or Japan, but, if the arduous task of grappling with this most sensitive problem must be undertaken, why not try to go beyond such limited action and solve the Security Council question on a really permanent basis?

Permanent membership in the Security Council, in contradiction to the principle of sovereign equality of all nations elsewhere adhered to in the Charter, has been based on what has proved to be a fleeting power constellation emerging from World War II. To adapt the concept now to the no less fleeting constellation emerging from the Vietnam War would not make the Council more permanent. What if—God forbid—India were to break up in the seventies under the pressure of economic, cultural, and linguistic problems?

What should and can be made permanent is a set of qualifications for choosing the decision-makers on the Security Council on whose unanimous consensus world security must be based, rather than relying on the identity or individuality of such members. These qualifications must include: a large population; a high level of economic-industrial development or gross national product; and a role, at least in recent history, that inspires the trust and confidence of the world community in matters affecting war and peace. The Security Council as a whole must be geographically representative of all areas and peoples and politically and economically balanced between communist, non-communist, and non-aligned nations. The composition of such a Security Council, whose actions would be based on the consensus of at least nine veto-holding powers, could be entrusted only to the U.N. General Assembly, which might elect the permanent members once every ten or twelve years.

On such a basis, the People's Republic of China would almost certainly be elected to a permanent Security Council position. Her political balance, geographical position, size of population, and gross national product would all warrant and make inevitable such a position. (Taiwan, after a period of transition and genuine self-determination, could qualify as a non-permanent member. She could do so if she chooses independence but, depending on the size of the Council, she could also conceivably do so even as an autonomous province of the People's Republic of China. In this case, Taiwan might play an international role analogous to that of Byelorussia on the Ukraine within the Soviet Union.)

The only remaining question would be China's role in recent history and whether this role inspires the trust and confidence of the world community. If we have two interpretations of the Lin Piao doctrine—as an interpretation of history or as a blueprint for Chinese action—I would unhesitatingly choose the former. The frequently repeated official Chinese declarations that revolutions cannot be exported and that each people must be responsible for its own revolution would seem to support this interpretation. The Chinese ambition to recover all the territories historically subject to the suzerainty of the Han people, however, cannot be ignored. The general, or generalizable, problem arising from China's demands for territorial reintegration is: How far back into the past may claims of this kind extend and when does the status quo determine an historically valid reality, the violation of which constitutes aggression? This question must be answered not only for China and Taiwan but for the two Germanies, for the Oder-Neisse frontier, for the Tyrol, and for Israel, to name only a few. The determination of the Chinese boundaries should follow a categorical imperative that would be applicable to other boundaries as well.

ALAN CRANSTON:

I believe that the major powers should not have such overpowering representation on the Security Council but that it should include more nations of moderate size. Not only Japan but India, Indonesia, and ultimately Germany perhaps have legitimate claims to Security Council representation. The Security Council might someday become analogous to the United States Senate, with a somewhat more limited membership.

Related to this problem is the question of finding a more equitable system than one-nation, one-vote in the General Assembly. The major powers will never permit the Assembly any real authority as long as tiny nations have equal voting power with great ones. At present the General Assembly fails to correlate the voice each country has in the United Nations with its size and its actual role in international affairs.

Long ago the head of one smaller Asiatic nation to whom I spoke told me: "We of the small nations would be more than willing to give up the fiction of equality in a United Nations that has no real authority to keep the peace, in favor of a vote equal to our world role, which is not great, in a United Nations with true peacekeeping ability."

Many suggestions have come forth from time to time, ranging from weighted representation derived from factors like literacy, economic power, and population to a simple formula based on population alone, with a ceiling and a basement. Whatever the solution, I believe a reallocation of voting power in the General Assembly is as urgent a question as the reorganization of the Security Council.

CHESTER A. RONNING:

I think we must be very careful in inviting China to join the United Nations not to give the impression that we are doing it to show her up if she does not accept. We of the West must remember that we have kept the Chinese out for twenty years this fall. If they take twenty years to accept our invitation to join, they will be no more unreasonable than we have been.

Also, in extending an invitation to China, we must take care not to lay the ground for reducing Chinese influence when she does come in. If and when China joins the United Nations we will no doubt find it difficult. But listening to Chinese opinions will be wholesome for us, as it has been to hear voices from Africa and other developing nations. We have ruled the roost for so long it is time for us to listen.

If, in our efforts to improve the Security Council, we should make designs now that will later prevent China from having a veto power or so enlarge the Security Council that China's influence will be diminished, China may refuse to join on these grounds. If she does, the blame will be ours, not hers.

EDWIN O. REISCHAUER:

Let me just warn against using the term, "two Chinas." China is not only the largest country in the world but the oldest. For hundreds of years at a time, China has not been unified, but she has been an integrated unit for the greater part of two millennia. The Chinese have a tradition, you might even call it a myth, of unity. To all Chinese the concept of two Chinas is an immoral idea. They all reject it, Nationalist and Communist alike. I think it is highly inappropriate for any foreigners, particularly Americans, to suggest that two Chinas is a solution to Chinese representation in the United Nations.

The Chinese have very subtle minds; they are a pragmatic people. Their present communist phase in many ways fits with their philosophical background because they have always had an idealistic philosophy. Their Confucianism has traditionally projected a great world order, the perfect system, but Chinese realities have seldom matched the theory. The Chinese historically have been able to accommodate ideal concepts and muddy, messy realities. In terms of China's past, the Chinese would not find it difficult to think of China as a unified nation while they somehow defined two different political entities, perhaps both of them in the United Nations. I think the Chinese themselves will have to discover the formula.

HARVEY WHEELER:

I hear it said repeatedly that Taiwan is a problem for China to solve, a domestic issue between Mao Tse-tung and Chiang Kai-shek, or perhaps even a matter to engage the concern of the Taiwanese.

America gave birth to the Taiwan problem and America must bury it. Without American aid and American support, Taiwan—or, more accurately, the exiled regime of Chiang Kai-shek—would have no place in the councils of the great powers.

Perhaps the United States can "internationalize" the problem by helping to place it, along with the Berlin and Israeli conflicts, under U.N. jurisdiction. Before we could make such a move, we would need to take the United Nations seriously and give it a true police force. I am not optimistic, however, since America fears a strong United Nations more than it fears the communist threat, and the socialist powers share our goal of keeping the United Nations weak.

IV

A
NEW AGE
FOR ASIA

"To know nothing but the art of waging war may make men efficient in actual combat, but it causes them to be totally lacking in general knowledge and the behavior proper to sensible citizens, which, in turn, leads them to meddle with assurance in fields beyond their ken."
Shigeru Yoshida

No matter what modifications the United States, the nations of Europe, the Soviet Union, and Japan may make in their Asian policies in the years to come, their course will depend on China. China's physical size, her huge population, and her geographical location leave the world no choice. Stretching from the heart of Eurasia across the top of the world to the Pacific Ocean, China spreads her influence to the east, west, north, and south. Events within isolated China cannot help but have their effect on the nations beyond.

Probably the most far-reaching and fundamentally disturbing development on the mainland is the Great Proletarian Cultural Revolution. As yet incomplete, its scope still unknown, the Cultural Revolution promises, even now, to rank among the great human upheavals of history. It baffles even those nations in close cultural and geographical proximity to China; for predominantly non-revolutionary Americans, its mystique is that it makes no sense. The Cultural Revolution, if it is to be appreciated, must be viewed both as a unique Chinese experience and as part of the revolutionary potential called upon throughout history by charismatic leaders of both East and West.

Both "Cultural" and "Revolution" have special meanings in Communist China. Culture denotes the political creed, the ideology as it is embodied in the leadership and enforced throughout society. In this special context, culture implies both a purity of concept and the power implicit in maintaining the ideal. Revolution has no connotation of political and social unrest or of mass protest. It is an upheaval decreed from above. "Purge," too, has a particular meaning in the Chinese application. A purged individual is held up as a dangerous example of impurity of thought, a "demon" or "monster" whose heresy threatens the life of the revolution. The attack upon the purged person has a highly symbolic, shadowy quality.

While it is distinctively Chinese in its various manifestations, the Cultural Revolution, in its symbolic qualities, has an affinity for the spirit of other great revolutions. Through its entire course runs the theme of rebirth. Mao has sought a restoration of the revolutionary fervor that transcends daily trials and brings men, high and low, into the immortal historical process. Swept up in the wave, ordinary men "dared command the sun and moon to bring a new day."

In the context of this theme, the youthful Red Guard, for all its transitory role, acquires a special symbolism, an embodiment of the dedication to renewal and perpetual life, an assertion of revolutionary immortality. Sweeping everything before it, the Red Guard cleansed the land of the old and the fading, leaving only the powerful vision of Mao and the purity of his Thought.

The merger of purity and power, with purity the supreme source of all power, is another theme of the Revolution. Here again, the Red Guard has a special significance, pure in its class origins, powerful agent of revolution. In both Western and Eastern cultures power has been god-given, the special property of the virtuous prince. In the Chinese tradition, Mao, the Leader, with his legacy, the Mandate of Heaven, has become the symbol of absolute virtue transcending human mortality.

Ideological totalism fits well with this theme, but more significant is the polarization between good and evil that totalism fosters. In the Cultural Revolution we have witnessed an extension of this simple opposition to involve the confrontation between being "red" and being "expert." In its political sense, the struggle between the "reds" and "the experts" may be the effort of fervent ideologists to prevent social stratification and the entrenchment of an elitist bureaucracy. By implication, the purity and power of Mao's Thought has been deemed the ultimate source of strength in all things, the "spiritual atom bomb," leaving no need for experts.

The logic that has centered all purity and omnipotent power in Mao, the virtuous leader, fuses the Man and his Thought into one all-nurturing force. The Man-Thought becomes a mythical hero, immortal even in life, through whom even the most insignificant can participate in history. Mao becomes the figure of destiny.

The aims of the Cultural Revolution may be purely local—an attempt to revitalize the internal government structure or a device to immortalize Mao Tse-tung, as has been claimed. The world, however, cannot escape the impact of internal events in a nation the size of China. The consolidation processes of modern nation-states exert pressures beyond their borders, particularly in the case of China. When the Cultural Revolution is finally done, the nations of the Pacific and of the world at large will deal with its results, not primarily in their internal terms, but in their external ramifications.

*"Neither canned prawns nor soy sauce /
May America's borders cross; /
Canadians, amazed, confused, / Are irritated and amused.*

*"Soy sauce endangers security, /
The reason's there for all to see. /
So deeply red it's purple nearly / —Criminal nature proven clearly.*

*"And as to Chinese big prawns canned, /
They obviously must be banned; /
In armor cased from tail to head, When boiled they turn a fiery red.*

*"An Iron Curtain America blinds, /
Hysteria grips the White House mind; / Strategic goods
—what if they're edible? / Such idiocy is scarcely credible."*
Yuan Shui-po

---

12   Trade and Development: Keys to Asian Stability

A DISCUSSION WITH:

William O. Douglas
Aiichiro Fujiyama
Edwin O. Reischauer
Harry S. Ashmore
Tokuma Utsunomiya
Yasumi Kurogane
Shunichi Matsumoto
Don Edwards
Chester A. Ronning
Munenori Akagi
John Sherman Cooper
Mark O. Hatfield
J.W. Fulbright
Stanley Sheinbaum
Arthur Goldberg

JUSTICE DOUGLAS: As many of you know, a constant complaint before the United Nations is that, apart from Japan, the Asian countries, as producers of raw materials, are at the mercy of Western buyers. Because the developing nations of Asia are unable to command productive prices for their goods or establish favorable trade balances, they argue strongly for the establishment of an Asian common market. Japan would be the logical leader of such an enterprise.

We in America could benefit from the experience of our Japanese colleagues. What are the Japanese views on a common market for Asia and on the larger questions of Asian trade and economic development?

MR. FUJIYAMA: In Asia the two major problems are poverty and economic underdevelopment; together they form the foundation of political instability. It follows that the solution to political unrest depends primarily on solutions to economic issues—finding ways for Asian countries to sell their primary agricultural products on the world market and providing the technological skills necessary for industrialization.

An Asian common market could result in lowered tariffs and in stronger economic ties among the countries of Asia, enabling them to avoid economic conflict with their neighbors and to create common interests. UNCTD, the United Nations Century of Trade Development, has discussed at some length how to provide markets for primary products, how to increase the volume of purchases, and how to lower the customs duties levied on the primary goods of developing countries. One organization, ECAFE, is working actively to develop coöperation in the economic sphere.

Japan is gravely concerned with the whole question of Asian development. She has recently deposited two hundred million dollars in the Asian Development Bank, an amount equal to the United States contribution; and one of the governors of the Bank is a Japanese. Instruments like the Asian Development Bank can fulfill a common-market function, and the aid thus provided will help to create a sound foundation for stability in the Far East.

The other problem is the industrialization of Asian countries. I believe Japan can play a big role in this area. During the Meiji era Japan began her own industrialization with small and medium industries and even today many still flourish. Therefore Japan has the knowledge and background to help developing countries establish an industrial base. Asia lacks trained personnel, and technological aid and education must consequently precede any significant industrial development or effort at modernizing agriculture.

Until now economic aid from the West has been concentrated on financing large, rather sophisticated factories. In Ceylon I once saw an expensive, modern ceramic plant that had been purchased from Switzerland. The only difficulty was that none of the Ceylonese had enough training to profit from this major investment by operating the plant at full capacity. They would have been much better off if they had asked for help in modernizing the pottery plant they already had. In Asia most countries need assistance in elementary technology, and I believe Asian industrial development should be tied to the daily lives of the people. From initial small projects, the nations of Asia can gradually move on to larger, more technical industry.

Japan has a difficult situation with regard to the products of developing countries. The advanced nations of the West suggest that Japan, as a highly industrialized unit, give more favorable treatment to the goods from developing nations. But the considerable number of small and medium plants in Japan would suffer from such a policy adjustment. We have not been able to open our doors entirely, and the developing countries voice their concern quite frequently. In the future I believe Japan must give more consideration to their demands and greater thought to ways of providing markets for her less developed neighbors.

AMBASSADOR REISCHAUER: I wonder how many people realize that Japan, through her contributions to the Asian Development Bank, is the only nation to match a major American aid effort since the Second World War.

MR. ASHMORE: Has Japan any technical missions in China now, or is the possibility under discussion?

MR. FUJIYAMA: We have one. Japan exported a synthetic fiber plant to China, and Japanese technicians are working with the Chinese in operating this plant.

I feel there is room for considerable expansion. In the past the Russians sent many hydroelectric plants to China. When the Soviets stopped exporting to the People's Republic, the French and the West Germans stepped into the breach. I believe that China would be interested in buying plants of this type from Japan, very interested.

MR. UTSUNOMIYA: The Chinese began taking a great interest in trade with Japan around 1956 when their relations with the Soviet Union were deteriorating. In Harbin I once saw a Chinese electrical generating plant designed for a capacity of about three hundred thousand kilowatts of power. This plant had been built with Soviet technical aid. Before the Russians withdrew, the Chinese were generating ten thousand kilowatts per hour, but after 1959 the operation stopped for nearly two years. Today, after much effort, China has hydroelectric plants of her own capable of generating three hundred thousand kilowatts.

China needs a great deal of fundamental help in improving the economic lot of her people. In the West we hear criticism of China's economic backwardness, but the present leaders of China are fully aware that their country is backward and are working hard to catch up. We must remember that five hundred million Chinese are farmers; the prime worry of the Chinese leaders is how to raise the agricultural level in their country. When I met with Chinese economists in 1961, they admitted that they were starting from an extremely low economic base. They pointed out that if Chinese farmers were to be supplied with nitrate fertilizers in the same measure that Japanese farmers use them, China would need fifty million tons annually. To produce this amount would take fifty years at China's present rate of production. Therefore China must import fertilizer for a long time, even if she begins to develop her own fertilizer industry—and she is anxious to do so.

China really has a great need to remain introspective so that she can develop and advance. If she is left alone, I feel that China will concentrate on domestic problems, but if she feels threatened, the whole political machinery will be directed outward.

MR. FUJIYAMA: I should explain that Japan has only one technical mission in China because the whole program of exporting entire plants to the continent has come to a halt. The government has refused to allow the Japan Export-Import Bank to make funds available to China on a deferred payment plan, in other words, on terms sufficiently favorable for the Chinese to be able to accept them.

MR. UTSUNOMIYA: We know that China has wanted for some time to step up a program of industrialization and recognizes that she must have outside resources to do so. That is the purpose of the industrial fairs in Peking and Shanghai. We Japanese want to exhibit equipment that could help China raise the living standard of her agrarian population. Unless the Japanese government changes its policy to permit deferred payments, however, we will not be able to export the industrial plants they need. The Western European nations do allow deferred payments, and so China will naturally deal with them. The most important stimulus needed for Japan-China trade is the release of funds from the Japan Export-Import Bank on competitive terms.

AMBASSADOR REISCHAUER: Several plants have been exported in the past to China by the Kurashiki Rayon Company and other private industries. Would a relaxation of the Export-Import Bank's restriction now contribute materially to increased trade? Would there be a sizable change in the whole trade relationship or only a small expansion?

MR. FUJIYAMA: A precise estimate is difficult, but I feel that we could expect quite a substantial increase. After the Kurashiki Company's successful venture, the Dai-Nippon Spinning Company tried to follow suit, but the government thwarted its efforts. Since then the government has forbidden the export of any plants financed by funds from the Export-Import Bank. I believe that the Chinese are interested in building more synthetic fiber plants; also, I think they offer a potential market for shipping, for steel, and for factory machinery.

MR. KUROGANE: I think that the exports Mr. Fujiyama mentioned—synthetic fibers, steel mills, and shipping—could substantially increase Japanese trade with China, but I expect that Communist China's preoccupation with her severe social problems will limit the potential market. China's seven to eight hundred million people seem like a vast market, but I do not expect any rapid industrial or economic growth on the continent to open up that market in the immediate future.

AMBASSADOR MATSUMOTO: The largest single item of trade in terms of money between Japan and China is fertilizer. We now export both ammonium sulfate and nitrate fertilizers to China. West Germany and Italy are Japan's competitors in this field. The great interest the Italians have in China, and, I suspect, the reason for Italy's desire to recognize the People's Republic, is that China is a market for Italian fertilizer. As a great agrarian country, China must at present import fertilizer, but the real need is for facilities to enable China to produce her own. In addition to the Kurashiki venture and the abortive attempts by the Dai-Nippon Spinning Company and the Hitachi Shipbuilding Company to export complete plants, the Japanese considered sending a urea factory to China. Blocked by the Import-Export Bank's credit policy, they were unable to go through with it. A Dutch company did, however, set up a urea plant that is now in full operation in the suburbs of Shanghai.

MR. FUJIYAMA: Perhaps some comparative statistics will help to explain Japan's enthusiasm for trade with China even though continental China probably cannot reach her full trading potential for some time.

Japan's exports to the United States total three billion dollars annually, for an average per capita consumption in the United States of fifteen dollars' worth of Japanese goods.

China now buys about $350 millions worth of Japanese goods annually, a per capita rate of about fifty cents. If financial restrictions were removed, I feel that Chinese per capita consumption could be doubled and perhaps pushed to two dollars a head. With China's huge population, the total expansion could move rapidly into the billions. The potential Chinese market, even now, could more than offset Japan's unfavorable half-million-dollar balance of trade with Australia—which can hardly be cured otherwise since Australia's per capita consumption of Japanese goods is already twice that of the United States.

MR. EDWARDS: The Japanese total balance of trade for 1968 was certainly not unfavorable; it was favorable by, I believe, over two billion dollars, with a balance-of-payments favorable in excess of a billion dollars. But I would like to ask—

MR. FUJIYAMA: Our trade balance with the United States was favorable but with Australia it was unfavorable.

MR. RONNING: Mr. Fujiyama could also mention Canada. Japan has a very unfavorable balance of trade with Canada.

MR. EDWARDS: Yes, I understand. But to continue, I believe that a Japanese trade mission went to Peking about a year ago and had problems with the Chinese government. I read that they finally reached an agreement but that the Chinese insisted upon a political statement from the Japanese delegation. My understanding is that the Japanese delegation accepted three political principles along with the commercial aspects of the agreement: one, that Japan would not take a hostile attitude toward China; two, that Japan would not take part in the "plot" to form two Chinas; and three, that Japan would not obstruct better Chinese-Japanese relations. The Japanese apparently felt that, as representatives of private organizations, they could sign such a document even though two Diet members were among their group. If my interpretation is correct, the Japanese are not being politically restricted in their trading by government policy as our merchants and investors are in the United States.

AMBASSADOR MATSUMOTO: I know a little about this since I was a member of the delegation that arranged the first Japan-China trade agreement six or seven years ago.

The Japanese government could never have formally accepted the three principles you mentioned. Japanese trade with China has been accomplished through two kinds of non-governmental, private arrangements, the L-T agreements and the "friendship trade." The guiding principle of Japan-China trade has been the separation of economics from political affairs, a formula arrived at during the administration of Hayato Ikeda.

The L-T agreements were arranged by Kenzo Matsumura and Tatsunosuke Takasaki with a high Chinese party official, Liao Ch'eng-chi. "L" stands for Liao and "T" for Takasaki, who was a member of Japan's lower house. The L-T agreements outlined a general plan for Japan-China trade between 1963 and 1967, with many concrete arrangements to be negotiated separately. The terms of these trade programs were usually complex. The original L-T agreements expired in 1967; now the terms must be renegotiated annually.

In the other type of arrangement, the so-called friendship trade, Japanese private firms regarded by China as "friendly toward the Peking regime" have made a number of makeshift deals with Chinese trade organizations. The volume of "friendship trade" is not sufficient to satisfy the trading ambitions of Japanese businessmen, but it has the advantage that it can continue even if the L-T agreements break down.

I suspect that the Japanese government wishes the L-T trade to continue because of its obvious advantage to the Japanese economy. Thus, although the government, under the formula of the separation of economics and politics, gave no official cognizance to the three political principles enunciated by the Chinese, it gave them passive recognition by abstaining from protest.

MR. UTSUNOMIYA: One major problem in Japanese-Chinese

trade relations is the refusal of the Japanese Ministry of Agriculture to permit the import of Chinese beef. Whether this prohibition is for purely technical reasons, as the government maintains, or whether politics influences the decision, I do not know.

AMBASSADOR MATSUMOTO: Beef is expensive and scarce in Japan, and before the war we used to buy Chinese beef. Today the Japanese government claims that Chinese cattle have hoof-and-mouth disease. This claim is disputed by the Chinese, and many Japanese do not believe it. Whatever the case, the beef issue needs immediate settlement. Renegotiation of the L-T agreements has been made difficult because Japan's Ministry of Agriculture has so far failed to come up with a clear explanation of its prohibition on Chinese beef, and China finds the whole controversy irritating.

MR. AKAGI: Since I was at one time Minister of Agriculture, I would like to offer a few comments. As you know hoof-and-mouth disease is dangerous. In Great Britain thousands of head of cattle have been slaughtered to prevent the spread of this disease, and the United States banned imports of beef from Argentina because of it. When Argentina protested strongly, the United States began importing boiled Argentine beef. Japan has followed suit. I myself negotiated the agreement to expedite Japanese import of boiled Argentine beef.

Japan cannot import raw beef from China without assurances that hoof-and-mouth disease is not present. So far, the Chinese have failed to provide convincing assurances. International agreements covering quarantine of animals suspected of hoof-and-mouth disease are in effect, and if China were a member of the international community of nations and were participating in these agreements on the export of live animals, Japan could accept her assurances. Of course, understanding the difficulty does not offer us an immediate solution to the problem, but it does point up the urgency of bringing China into international society.

PROFESSOR NEAL: I would be interested to know whether

or not you feel that the attitude of the American government has had an impact on Chinese-Japanese trade.

MR. UTSUNOMIYA: We know that the Japanese government's attitude affects Japan-China trade, but we do not know just how much influence the United States has on the Japanese government. Many Japanese feel that government policy is greatly influenced by U.S. attitudes. However, before the Kurashiki plant was approved, I met with Mr. Roger Hilsman, who was then in the State Department. Mr. Hilsman assured me that the United States had no intention of hindering Japan-China trade. He said that as long as Japan did not give preferential treatment to China, that is to say, deferred payments on better terms than those to other Asian countries, the United States would not raise any protest.

SENATOR COOPER: I believe that the smallest step the United States should take would be to encourage our allies and the neutral countries to trade with China instead of actively discouraging them. Increased trade would create mutual interest between the countries engaged in it, would open up more complexities for Communist China to deal with, and thus would bring China more into the community of nations.

MR. EDWARDS: If the United States itself were to open up trade with Communist China, the Pacific Coast would reap most of the benefit, particularly the port cities of Seattle, San Francisco, and Los Angeles. China's chief imports—wheat, chemical fertilizer, and industrial equipment—are all available for sale on the West Coast, and the rapidly expanding population of the western states would provide an appropriate market for the cotton fabrics, simple consumer goods, and light industrial products of China. The advantages to the West Coast economy of an increased Asian trade have long been recognized by Pacific Coast businessmen.

The opening of trade with China would not currently be a large item in American commercial accounts. China is still primarily an underdeveloped, agrarian nation with a per capita income of eighty-five dollars (as compared with Japan's

$922 per person). Present Chinese imports are under two billion dollars a year. United States exports in 1966 alone were $30.4 billions, with $5.7 billions to Canada, $7.5 billions to Western Europe, $3 billions to Japan, and $179 millions to Russia and other communist countries. At the present time China provides a modest market. What it will amount to in the future will depend on many factors that concern only the Chinese and their ability to create a modern nation.

Tentative suggestions for trade with China are heard now and then from world trade organizations, shipping associations, and waterfront-employer groups. So far these proposals have been advanced without force and quickly withdrawn or forgotten when greeted with hostility from the State Department. Such suggestions are likely to become more frequent now that America's comfortable trade surpluses have been reduced so drastically. In 1968 United States exports showed a surplus of approximately $1 billion, compared to $4.1 billions in 1967. If the trend continues downward into a steady deficit, the vision of 750,000,000 potential Chinese customers could stimulate American companies to exert the same kind of effective pressure in Washington that Japanese companies apply so successfully in Tokyo. As Americans continue to have a harder time selling their goods abroad, the prospect of new markets will appeal to American businessmen, and the Nixon Administration consists primarily of American businessmen.

SENATOR HATFIELD: As many people have pointed out, our isolation of Peking by a trade embargo is entirely symbolic. It has not lessened the amount of goods that the Chinese are capable of importing and exporting, but it has served as a symbol of our hostile attitude. Many of our allies in the West have rejected our self-defeating policies and trade freely with China. Whereas in the early years of the People's Republic most of Peking's trade was with other communist nations, today approximately seventy-five per cent of her trade is with the West.

SENATOR FULBRIGHT: I do not see any reason for us not to encourage other countries to trade with China and even to extend her long-term credit. China now does most of her trading with our major allies—the United Kingdom, Japan, West Germany, Australia, Canada, Italy, and France. Our attempt at embargo has had little economic effect, but it has certainly helped to embitter our relations with China and has done nothing to enhance our reputation in Chinese eyes.

AMBASSADOR REISCHAUER: I agree that the United States should drop its economic embargo on trade with China and be ready to exchange non-strategic goods on the same basis that we trade with the Soviet Union. Our embargo has been absolutely meaningless. Beyond that, it is to our long-range interest and in keeping with our concept of international relations to encourage China's trade with America and the other advanced democracies.

However, I think the whole story of credit for plant exports illustrates clearly that the problem Japan faces is with Taiwan and not with the United States. I do not deny that a few years ago many of us in the government suggested mildly from time to time to the Japanese that they might find it more in their interest to extend soft terms of credit to trading partners with more or less amenable economies, such as the nations of Southeast Asia and India. But I have a clear memory of the Kurashiki Rayon Plant proposal, and we made no such suggestion in that case. However, rumors became common in Japan that the United States was trying to block the sale of the fiber plant to China. This so disturbed Mr. Soichiro Ohara, President of Kurashiki, that he came to me, and I assured him that the United States was in no way opposed to the sale of the rayon plant.

Taiwan raised such an uproar over this evidence of improving Japan-China trade, however, that Mr. Shigeru Yoshida paid an informal visit to Taiwan to smooth relations. Mr. Yoshida was not in the government at the time, but he was a prestigious former Prime Minister and was, in a sense, acting in an official capacity. Mr. Yoshida's visit resulted in a promise not to use the credits of the Import-Export Bank to underwrite the export of plants in the future, the so-called Yoshida letter.*

The United States took no stand on the credit issue except

one of friendliness to Japan's economic interests, while Taiwan took strong exception to Prime Minister Ikeda's trade policy. The Japanese reacted to Taiwan. The problem the Japanese face in their relations with China is not the United States; it is Taiwan.

MR. KUROGANE: Yes, Ambassador Reischauer is correct. Hitachi Light Industry and Dai-Nippon Textile wanted to export plants to China, but Taiwan voiced such strong opposition that Japanese policy was reversed and Japan issued the Yoshida letter.

MR. SHEINBAUM: I'm curious to know why Taiwan's pressure was so successful. Was it a matter of trade?

AMBASSADOR REISCHAUER: May I give you some statistics to illustrate the pressure that Taiwan can exert on Japan? As near as I can remember, during 1967, the last full year we have for foreign trade, Japanese trade with Communist China totaled about $560 millions, a decline from $620 millions the year before, perhaps because of the Cultural Revolution. That year Japanese trade with Taiwan was approximately $450 millions, about four-fifths as much as her total volume with mainland China.

Over and above trade, Japanese capital has been flowing into Taiwan in increasing amounts in recent years. As Japan continues to build up Taiwan, she is, in a sense, building a greater and greater problem in her relations with China.

AMBASSADOR GOLDBERG: Apparently Japan and Taiwan are substantial trading partners. In the light of Taiwan's known political attitudes, how can this trade be reconciled with the moves that Japan is making toward mainland China? Is it possible to carry water on both shoulders in this complex, emotional, difficult situation vis-à-vis Taiwan?

AMBASSADOR REISCHAUER: Basically Japan has followed a policy of maximizing economic contact and minimizing political involvements. So far this has been a successful policy that the Japanese are reluctant to disturb.

AMBASSADOR MATSUMOTO: The Chinese believe that the separation of politics from economics is wrong, that politics and economics must be one. As a result, last year the L-T trade seemed on the verge of collapse. At least, China gave that impression to the outside world. Mr. Kenzo Matsumura made great efforts to keep the agreements alive; I accompanied him to Peking. In February, 1968, Mr. Tagawa and Mr. Shiga, both long-time members of the Liberal Democratic Party, together with Mr. Kaheita Okazaki, one of the principal pillars of Japan-China trade, spent roughly one month in Peking negotiating with the Chinese. The result was their agreement to the three political principles the Chinese advanced and the renewal of the agreements.

China has been obstructive lately with regard to the L-T agreements. The Peking leaders do not like the attitude of the Japanese government and have been throwing obstacles in the path of continuing the L-T arrangement. Mr. Yoshimi Furui, heading a four-man Japanese delegation, signed a new agreement with Peking last April covering the current year, but it was a drastically reduced, unsatisfactory agreement.

MR. FUJIYAMA: Taiwan is not the only difficulty in Japanese trade relations with China. China's own internal policies are also a barrier. Japan's trade with China before the war consisted mainly of individual necessities. Today China has imposed severe restrictions on consumer goods, such as making all of her people wear black cotton clothes. I believe there can be no expansion in the market for daily necessities as long as these restrictions continue in effect.

MR. UTSUNOMIYA: Another problem is the ban on the export of strategic goods to communist countries, the so-called Co-Com Agreement, drawn up by the Coördinating Committee of the Consultative Group of NATO. As you know, I was president of the recently cancelled Japanese Industrial Fair, which was to have been held in Shanghai and Peking. One of my difficulties was the Co-Com Agreement. The Chinese have somehow managed to learn electronic technology. But electronic items are banned under the Co-Com stipulations, and we cannot export them to China. Sweden is not among the Co-Com nations, and much electronic equipment is reaching China through Sweden. Also, the French, the English, and the Italians are exporting many items that the Japanese government bans. The Japanese government is much stricter than many Western governments in applying Co-Com regulations. I do not know whether the United States insists on this stringent attitude on Japan's part, but I hope not. My own belief is that the United States is not hindering Japan-China trade.

AMBASSADOR REISCHAUER: In the long run the Japanese will have to take the initiative in broadening trade relations with China just as Japan will have to lead the way politically in bringing China back into the community of nations. The Japanese have more economic and cultural relations with China than any other people in the world; the Chinese pay more attention to them. They are in the best position to take the lead. I hope they will and that we can follow it.

---

*This letter is not to be confused with a letter written by Mr. Yoshida to Secretary of State John Foster Dulles in 1952, setting forth Japan's attitude on the recognition of Communist China and on the prospects for a peace treaty with Taiwan.

"Many of the winds of change in the modern world have swept out of Asia. Rich historical records and material furnish eloquent proof of the fact that Asian history has its brilliant and important place in the history of world civilization."
Liu Tan-nien

13

The Importance of Cultural Exchange

A STATEMENT BY
Masumi Ezaki

THE IMPORTANCE OF CULTURAL EXCHANGE

MASUMI EZAKI:

Nation-states have begun only recently to appreciate the value of cultural exchange as a vital arm of foreign policy. The last years of the nineteenth century saw cultural exchange take vague shape as a supplement to diplomatic communication, but not until the mid-forties did it come into its own as a primary method of diminishing misunderstanding and enhancing mutual appreciation between geographically separated peoples. Sudden and accelerating advances in mass communications and transportation were the catalysts in the rush of cultural-exchange activity following the Second World War. Through the printed media, the graphic arts, and vastly improved radio, television, and recording techniques, nations far distant from each other could begin to close the cultural gap between them.

Culture represents the mode of life and forms of expression developed by a race or community in its struggle to rise from barbarism to the ideal state. It embraces all material and spiritual elements in the environment of any homogeneous group. The culture is expressed in various forms, including eating and living habits as well as such recognized cultural expressions as literature, music, art, dance, athletics, and religion. It extends to information-gathering and dissemination, learning and wisdom, science and technology.

Culture cannot be divorced from politics just as economics is unfailingly a part of political life, but true cultural exchange bears no relation either to nationalistic propaganda or to aggressive cultural suppression of one nation by another. To be successful, cultural exchange must mutually enrich the participating nations, enhancing goodwill and adding to the accumulated knowledge of each country. Real cultural exchange presumes that each nation will serve the other, each adding new elements to the other's existing cultural base and at the same time enhancing its own confidence and racial consciousness.

Cultural exchange cannot flourish in either a restricted or an anarchic climate. It must respect the dignity of each of the peoples involved, but it requires freedom from the fetters of discrimination based on race, creed, sex, social position, or economic status. Cultural exchange by definition must take place between independent peoples and cannot exist between ruler and the ruled or conqueror and the conquered. Peace is a prerequisite to genuine exchange; war may lead to material advances within nations but cannot contribute to more than technical exchanges between them. Thus, for maximum benefit, free communications must develop bilaterally between nations at peace with one another, each seeking to learn the values of the other. Multilateral cultural exchange is a supplement to and an extension of bilateral exchange.

When we try to apply these general principles to the problem of opening cultural exchange between the United States and the People's Republic of China, we discover several immediate obstacles. Three fundamental conditions normally associated with successful exchange are lacking: a common mother tongue, a similar social system, and a history of mutual interest and exchange activities promoted by geographical proximity. Cultural exchange can be accomplished when none of these conditions prevails but, at the outset at least, considerable difficulty is to be anticipated.

One solution to the problem of American-Chinese exchange might be for Japan to act as an intermediary in starting the cultural flow between the Eastern and the Western colossi. Japan's written language is sufficiently similar to the Chinese to provide the basis for communication, and the two countries are comparatively close in historical and cultural terms.

Chinese attitudes at present militate against their acceptance of even such uncontroversial American cultural forms as painting and sculpture. Chinese anti-Americanism extends to all aspects of American life, and China will not readily accept any American product. Nevertheless, since art forms are the most easily understood and do not depend on language for their appreciation, they would probably be useful in initiating exchange between the two countries. In this area,

Japan could perform a real service by supplying the setting for joint American and Chinese exhibitions and by providing the specialized historical and technical knowledge helpful to their appreciation.

Once the barriers have been broken down, exchange of personnel may be possible. The most likely American candidates for initial efforts would be scholars and theologians already known to the Chinese by reputation or through prior contact. Japan's role in effecting the first exchanges could be to sound out the Chinese and arrange whatever compromises are necessary. The next step would be an exchange of journalists, a long jump in the present inhospitable climate, and finally would come the formal exchange of ministers and ambassadors. Visionary as these latter steps may seem at present, rumors are already circulating that when the Cultural Revolution ends, Peking intends to dispatch large numbers of ambassadors and ministers abroad.

The United States has for many years conducted a vigorous and thoroughgoing exchange program with Japan in such fields as education, journalism, library techniques, and public information. Not all of the projects America has found successful in Japan would be appropriate in China. By the same token, many of the joint cultural projects now being pursued between Japan and mainland China would not be suitable for Chinese-American exchange. Current Japanese-Chinese activities could, however, provide guidelines for some United States-China cultural exchange in the future.

Japan initiated a cultural exchange program with Communist China in 1953 and formed the Japan-China Cultural Exchange Association in 1956. In 1959 an agreement between this association and the Chinese People's Association for Cultural Relations and Friendship with Foreign Countries provided the basis for systematic exchange. Since then cultural exchange has played a valuable role in renewing traditional Sino-Japanese friendship.

Exchange has been pursued in six major areas—sports, theater, art, literature, photography, and publications—and in several supplemental fields such as film-making and professor and student exchange. In the last ten years, twelve Japanese literary delegations have visited China and four

Chinese groups have come to Japan. Theatrical troops, including *kabuki, shigeki,* ballet, and light opera ensembles, have made a total of ten trips to China; in return Peking has sent drama, singing and dancing, and acrobatic groups to the Japanese islands. Art exhibitions exchanged between the two countries have included displays of ancient fine arts, pottery, painting, wood-block prints, photography, and calligraphy. Japanese camera teams have visited China on several occasions, and one especially successful venture was the filming by Iwanami Movie Productions of various aspects of the Cultural Revolution, a 35 millimeter color documentary now available in Japanese, English, and French.

Japanese and Chinese publishing companies have collaborated in making available several literary and artistic volumes, among the finest of which are the three volumes, *Arts of China,* a part of Hodansha Publishing Company's twenty-nine volume series, Outline of the World's Fine Arts. China provided all the photographs for these three volumes, each of which has recently been translated into English. In addition many Japanese-language periodicals like *People's China, China Graphic,* and *Peking Weekly* are regularly published in China.

Unlike exchanges in other fields, athletic exchange is restricted by the regulations of the International Olympics committee, which forbids member countries to meet with non-member nations. Under these regulations, Japan-China track and field meets are impossible, but some athletic exchange has been accomplished. Communist China is a member of the international federation governing volleyball, table tennis, gymnastics, skating, ice hockey, and tennis, and exchange has therefore been possible in these sports.

Much remains to be accomplished in furthering cultural exchange between Japan and China. We have made a beginning, but ultimate achievement of full exchange programs will depend on the normalization of diplomatic relations between the two countries. Once again, therefore, we are faced with resolving the central question and with finding ways and means to change the unyielding stance of the Japanese government, which refuses officially to recognize the People's Republic of China.

> *"The time has come to face the facts, not the myths. Objective observations, candor, and understanding are now more desirable than ever."*
> Shigeru Matsumoto

---

14 The Prospects for the Future

AN INTERROGATION WITH
Aiichiro Fujiyama

A CONVERSATION WITH:

Tokuma Utsunomiya
Ryohei Tamura
Mark O. Hatfield
Masumi Ezaki
John Sherman Cooper
Chester Ronning
Robert M. Hutchins

QUESTION: Do the Japanese believe that a United States military withdrawal from the western Pacific would result in a renewed outbreak of hostilities in Korea and expose Japan to the risk of involvement?

MR. FUJIYAMA: While I admit that the animosity between North and South Korea threatens constantly to flare into a new war, I do not believe that a United States military withdrawal from the Far East would necessarily precipitate an outbreak of fighting. Nor do I believe that renewed hostilities on the Korean peninsula would inevitably spread into an all-out war. If the elements that can cause war are present and are not resolved, fighting will resume regardless of the American presence, but I do not believe that present conditions will lead to such an impasse. Although United States military aid to South Korea helps to keep the situation inflamed, the Chinese and the Soviet Union have withdrawn the active support from North Korea that brought about a major confrontation in 1950.

A divided Korea will always threaten Asian stability, but the answer to the Korean problem is to locate and tackle the difficulties causing a lack of rapport between the two sections of the country. One hopeful sign is the current trend toward improvement in U.S.-Soviet relations. If the United States and the Soviet Union work out more coöperative relationships and if peaceful coexistence becomes more positive, the situation in Korea and in the Far East in general should correspondingly improve.

QUESTION: Would the withdrawal of American forces from the Far East result in Japanese rearmament, including nuclear armament?

MR. FUJIYAMA: Article IX of the Japanese Constitution, the peace clause, has taken deep root in the hearts of the Japanese people. The majority by far have a fundamental antipathy to rearmament, particularly to nuclear armament. I cannot conceive of Japan's rearming beyond the level of a self-defense force. A few Japanese do advocate rearmament, but when the Vietnam War ends and tension in East Asia falls off as a consequence, I confidently expect their protestations to die down to an insignificant murmur.

QUESTION: Do the other Asian nations trust the Americans militarily more than they do the Japanese? And do they believe Japanese rearmament would lead to another round of Japanese imperialism and aggression?

MR. FUJIYAMA: I would not attempt to assess the degree of distrust the nations of Asia feel toward Japan and the United States. To put it bluntly, neither nation enjoys full trust in Asia. The people of both countries would do well to join in efforts to improve their image among the Asians.

QUESTION: If we assume the hypothesis that war in Korea and Japanese rearmament would follow a U.S. military withdrawal, would the Japanese prefer American withdrawal even at such a high cost, or would they prefer a continued American military presence in the far Pacific?

MR. FUJIYAMA: I cannot answer the question except to reiterate what I have said about Korea and about Japanese rearmament because I do not accept the hypothesis. However, several corollary questions come to mind: Can there be stability if the United States continues a military presence in the Far East? And would the Chinese accept an American presence under any condition? Can the United States force acceptance on China?

I think that most Japanese reject the concept that peace can be maintained by military force alone. For example, whatever vacuum is created by the pending withdrawal of Great Britain from Asia can be filled, I sincerely believe, by economic efforts to improve the living standards of the region.

I could not bring myself personally to approve a continuing American military presence in Asia, and I do not think that China would ever voluntarily accept it. Can America force Chinese acceptance? Temporarily, perhaps, but force can never be a stable basis for permanent peace.

If peaceful intercourse is achieved, military measures will become obsolete. International coöperation can be pursued through better use of the United Nations, through greater reliance on the International Court of Justice, or through greater dependence upon formal and informal conferences among nations, industrialists, and cultural groups.

We in Japan are fortunate. Our constitution requires us to seek alternatives to military force in solving international disputes. Japan has officially renounced war as an extension of diplomacy, and her people believe that for Japan to rearm and to go to war again would do nothing to solve the problems in Asia today.

THE CONVERSATION

MR. UTSUNOMIYA: Today when tension over security and U.S.-Japanese relations is gripping Japan, the China problem looms larger than ever as a source of friction in Japanese internal affairs. The great majority in Japan support the Liberal Democratic Party, as they have ever since the end of the occupation. Many of those who vote for opposition candidates disagree violently with Liberal Democratic foreign policy; and it is significant that approximately half of the party's supporters favor improved relations between Japan and China.

Those of us in the Diet who argue for a liberalized foreign policy, particularly for a more rational approach to mainland China, form a minority faction in the Liberal Democratic Party, but, paradoxically, our views reflect the majority opinion in the country on this issue. The Japanese people are more liberal than the party they have elected to power, and opinions within the party itself are less conservative than those of the executive leadership.

As the date for renewal of the United States-Japan Security Treaty draws near, the government must make every effort to find a reasonable solution to the China problem. My great worry is that this outstanding flaw in its foreign policy will cost the ruling party the support of the general public.

MR. TAMURA: The Japanese people, as I understand them, are sick of the fighting that wracks the world. They have known defeat in a major war, and their history proves to them that military struggle leads to naught. While they recognize that American economic and military assistance has made Japan's remarkable postwar growth possible, the Japanese would still like to escape from a world dedicated to military solutions for every problem.

I, for one, would like from now on to think of the future and not of the past. How can Japan and America turn a new page in history? I propose that we start by changing our focus and reassessing our priorities. Let us stop thinking of people as communists and capitalists and consider them instead as individuals. Individual liberty and happiness, not ideologies or political designations, should be our concerns for the future.

The older generations today have no choice but to listen to the young, who will bear the burdens of the new age. Perhaps it is not possible for everyone in the world to become friends all at once, but we can devote our energies, as so many of our students ask, to beginning an international dialogue and to encouraging frank, free conversations among all nations.

Many of us believe that the election of President Nixon could mark the beginning of a new international era. He has an opportunity to introduce a refreshing mood of receptivity to change into foreign policy issues and to build bridges of friendship between the United States and China.

If my understanding is correct, the American politicians who advocate modification in United States China policy are in the minority in their country. I believe that politicians who dissent from their government's stand, both in Japan and in the United States, must have the courage to stand and fight for what they believe to be right. Only in this way can we make progress and cure the illness that inevitably afflicts any nation that accumulates too much economic or military power.

SENATOR HATFIELD: We may be in the minority, but I believe we can turn our minority status into a majority position by developing a strategy for peace. A strategy for peace calls for knowledge, shrewd tactics, and careful planning.

The effort to reconstitute American public opinion in support of a foreign policy based on understanding rather than on fear will involve a twofold approach. In the first place, I think that political leaders have an obligation to create public opinion rather than merely to reflect it. American public attitudes on foreign policy have been molded by the pronouncements of Secretaries Acheson, Dulles, and Rusk. The American people have heard relatively few powerful voices in dissent, and their opinions reflect the paucity of their information.

Secondly, I believe that those Americans who desire a change in foreign policy have a responsibility to express their opinions in their local communities. When a delegation calls on me in Washington, my first question usually is: "What have you done to influence your home-town editor and the business leaders and professional men in your community?"

President Nixon, like other Presidents before him, will not make radical moves if his political sense tells him that they will meet with strong public disapproval.

MR. EZAKI: In Japan we have a saying: "Let the waters wash it away." During the Cuban missile crisis a youthful American President confronted a wily, old, egocentric politician. President Kennedy, by virtue of his understanding and his vigor, averted a major war. The Japanese would say that he washed the crisis away with water.

Today in China we find an egocentric regime led by a hostile old revolutionary, Mao Tse-tung. In the United States a youthful new President has taken office, with all the wealth and power of the greatest nation on earth behind him. The opportunity is once again at hand for a rising American leader to wash away the egocentrism of a hostile regime with magnanimity and to accept China into the comity of nations.

SENATOR HATFIELD: Let us remind ourselves that Mr. Nixon is a minority President, elected by only forty-three per cent of the popular vote. His political victory was built on conservative southern votes together with those of the hard-liners on foreign policy questions. Majority public support must accompany any realistic United States policy, foreign or domestic. I question whether President Nixon has the running room in foreign policy so often attributed to him.

SENATOR COOPER: I am afraid I do not agree with my Republican colleague. As an elected official, Mr. Nixon will indeed have an instinctive sensitivity to public opinion, but I read American attitudes a little differently than Senator Hatfield.

I believe that Mr. Nixon's election reflects the desire of the American people to break out of our long-term foreign-policy pattern. Mr. Nixon has the tragic eight-year impasse in Vietnam before him, and he has listened to the rising public dissatisfaction with that war. Political considerations alone would dictate that he try to settle the Vietnam War, and a settlement there could in itself lead to a modification of American China policy.

Certainly, Mr. Nixon must deal with extremists on the Right who may press for escalation once more, but he has the advantage of a wide spectrum of opinion both in the country and within his own party. We must remember that one of his campaign statements was that we could not leave China forever outside the world community and that a dialogue must begin within the next two Presidential terms.

AMBASSADOR RONNING: The United States need not tackle the most difficult problems first. The important step would be for America to start negotiating, not to win a battle in the Cold War but to allay the Chinese fear of the United States. I do not understand why China has this fear, but I know that she harbors a fatalistic terror of American attack. The Chinese are preparing themselves to meet it. If the United States could hold out a hand and try to initiate negotiations toward a common purpose, little by little the fear may be dispelled and the way prepared for reaching solutions in the difficult areas.

MR. EZAKI: When you visit China you notice a terrible incongruity. Do you know what the Chinese characters for the United States are? They are *mei kuo,* meaning "the beautiful country."

Wall posters plastered everywhere in China describe the actions of the beautiful country in harsh, hostile terms, a remarkable contradiction. I have a feeling that the intractible language betrays China's deep resentment of an America that has spurned her in international circles. A friendly show of interest on the American side might bring to the fore once more the ancient concept of the beautiful country in the minds of the Chinese people.

SENATOR HATFIELD: Although I have said that I think we must develop a two-fold strategy for peace, my mind has been groping for exact formulas. How do I, as one American citizen and politician, implement my convictions? How do I share? How do I become an instrumentality for thawing the frozen American responses?

When Mr. Tamura was speaking of the Japanese young people, I caught the thread of an idea. Perhaps political leaders do not bear the sole responsibility for communicating with their counterparts abroad. If we can somehow devise a method to bring the young, the amateurs, into a dynamic effort to improve international communications, we can come closer to the ideal. Students, with their great adventuresome spirit, their lack of cynicism, and their faith, do not know enough to feel that friendship and understanding on a world scale are Utopian concepts. Their participation could provide needed impetus to the bridge-building that will bring together all the peoples living on the various sides of the great Pacific lake.

MR. UTSUNOMIYA: No matter how wealthy and powerful a nation may become, it will lose its influence if it loses its high moral sense. Both Japanese and Americans who are seeking a better relationship with China speak of themselves as being in a minority. I believe it is an honor to be among a minority whose convictions spring from conscience rather than to be with a majority that acts from purely political or economic motives.

One of Japan's Prime Ministers, Tanzan Ishibashi, once impressed the Chinese leaders with his earnestness when he declared that he would be willing to see Japan sacrificed if peace could thus be restored. Such moral dedication to peace is unfortunately all too rare today.

A threat or a menace is different from a natural disaster. Threats are man-made and can be removed by the efforts of men. Even if Communist China is indeed a menace, which I doubt, she certainly should not be treated like a natural disaster by either Japan or the United States.

AMBASSADOR RONNING: I find myself tremendously encouraged by the attitudes of so many Japanese. When I was Canadian High Commissioner to India, I saw the remarkable Japanese accomplishments in helping the people there to increase their agricultural production. In Southeast Asia their approach has been similar and the results as encouraging.

I have no doubt that Japan has the greatest ability of any nation to take the first step in resolving the problems of Asia by hammering out a working agreement with China. I only hope that nothing, not the United States nor even Taiwan, will hold the Japanese back.

MR. UTSUNOMIYA: I have two basic questions on the attitude of the American government and of the American people. If, for the sake of Japan or of the United States or of Asia in general, the American government were to decide to withdraw its forces from the far Pacific, would the American people accept the decision? And if Japan were to find a way to establish peace in the Far East through some non-military approach, would the United States accept and coöperate in the agreement?

MR. HUTCHINS: The United States is the most powerful country in the world and the one where there is the least danger, I should think, either internally or externally of an overthrow of the system. Suppose that the official policy of the United States were taken from the pages of a volume on world law rather than from the bloodiest pages in history. Might there not be a possibility of getting somewhere in establishing universal peace?

How do you get the American people behind a policy like this? You do it by holding hearings in the Senate, by talking, and by holding meetings and letting the public hear and read the conversations. Eventually, perhaps, you have some effect.

If the official policy of the United States on the China issue could be changed, wouldn't that be the greatest single contribution?

"The world is now waiting for us to reapply the faith we inherited from our fathers and to give it a new creative validity in the unchartered world that surrounds us. The road ahead, to be sure, is a hard road that man has never traveled before, a road full of great obstacles. But America has never long faltered in the face of new challenges."
John F. Kennedy

15 Fresh Approaches to Ancient Problems

A NEW REALISM FOR AN OUTWORN RATIONALITY

A STATEMENT BY
J. W. Fulbright

ASIATIC UNION

A STATEMENT BY
Harvey Wheeler

RECIPE FOR SURVIVAL: AN UNTRIED APPROACH IN AN UNPRECEDENTED AGE

A STATEMENT BY
William O. Douglas

A NEW REALISM FOR
AN OUTWORN RATIONALITY

J. W. FULBRIGHT:

The pattern of recurring militarism in international affairs is as old as history itself. Never has any country, large or small, successfully challenged the ancient belief that war is a normal extension of diplomacy. For many, many centuries military balance of power has been the only so-called rational approach to international relations. Any fair-sized country could always get away with robbing its neighbors. Until now.

Not long ago American scientists discovered the hydrogen bomb, and other nations understood its secrets a short time later. From that moment forward, a little country could destroy a giant power. The world entered a new era; an attempt by any nation to follow ancient policies based on the old rationality would thenceforth carry the risk of almost instant worldwide disaster.

The hydrogen bomb is not just another weapon, as some have held. It is an instrument of total destruction. In the atomic age the use of nuclear power to settle disputes becomes utterly irrational, and traditional concepts are little more than emotional hangovers from bygone days. Perhaps the human race, having proved over thousands of years the bankruptcy of force as an instrument of policy, has finally reached a point where it will use reason rather than might to effect solutions to international problems.

Japan is unique in the world today. A strong, growing nation, one of the most powerful economically despite her small size, Japan's traditions of virility and unity boast a history nearly as long as China's. In modern times this island nation has demonstrated remarkable energy and resourcefulness. Yet, except for a relatively small defense force (limited by her postwar Constitution), Japan is without arms. She has a minimum investment in a military machine. Her situation is unprecedented in the annals of history.

The United States has made an inconceivably large investment in the Pentagon and the military establishment. This year the Congress appropriated eighty billion dollars for defense, a sum larger than the total Japanese budget. America is exhausting itself by sinking its wealth into an unproductive activity, an investment in destructive capability that cannot bring back to our society anything of value.

We are accustomed to think of wealth in terms of gross national product. What really do we mean when we in America point with pride to our immense G.N.P.? Are we speaking of our basic assets, which are smaller than Russia's, or are we boasting of that large part of our wealth devoted exclusively to advertising and cosmetics? When I reflect that so much of our energy has been devoted to frivolous consumption and somber arms production, I am suspicious of gross national product as a measure of wealth.

It is commonly said that the United States has a duty to maintain its fleet in the Far East to fill the vacuum that will be left when Great Britain withdraws. Where *is* this vacuum? After all, people *live* there. I believe that if Americans went home and behaved themselves, these people would be quite likely to conduct their affairs in an orderly way. By what god-given right were the British there in the first place, or the Japanese either, except to patrol their own territory? I see no reason for the United States to feel any responsibility to fill a vacuum that is not there.

Japan's unique postwar development gives her an unparalleled opportunity to take an initiative never before available to any country in history. As a rich, dynamic nation with a negligible military investment, Japan could change the whole current of world thinking by taking a new, *modern* approach to international issues. She could start with China and say to that great, emerging Asian power: "Look! All the great nations of the world are breaking themselves in an arms race leading to universal disaster. This is absurd. Japan is not going to rearm. We want to take a peaceful approach to our mutual dilemmas, and we expect you to reciprocate."

How great would be the risk? Much less, in my opinion, than the road to rearmament would entail. Japan is an American ally. With the enormous militarization of the United States, why should anyone need more arms? The United States has enough for all, enough to kill each person in the world ten times over.

A dedication to peace in times of international crisis is called visionary by hardheaded modern leaders, but it may be the only realistic path still open. In a nuclear world, the traditional military approach can lead, I believe, only to certain destruction. The Japanese are an ancient people to whom Americans must seem relatively young and inexperienced. If the Japanese were willing to wrench themselves loose from ancient concepts and to venture in a new, non-military direction, they might lead the way to world salvation and encourage others to follow. The vehicle for a coöperative world structure, the United Nations, is already in being. Perhaps Japan can help us to use it.

ASIATIC UNION

HARVEY WHEELER:

Sixty years ago France, Britain, and Germany were the world's greatest powers and Europe the hub of civilization. In those times power was measured by size, strength, and colonial possessions. This was proclaimed the end intended by history, and Russia, China, Japan, and India evoked only disdain—sloughs of underdevelopment, cradles of serfdom, or both.

Twenty-five years and two world wars later, the glories of European civilization were gone as a cultural force. The quaint little nation-states that survived scrimped and struggled to keep pace with the two superpowers whose leaders played only table-stakes politics.

Two decades went by. When Richard Nixon finally won the American Presidency, the world was no longer bipolar. The long-standing capitalist-communist controversy had lost its comfortable familiarity. There were too many different kinds of Reds in the world, and some of them hated each other even more than they hated capitalists or than capitalists hated them. For one faction in Europe, the new socialist radicalism was but the old market mechanism writ large. Meanwhile, in the Far East, another breed of socialist radicals seemed to be saying that Tom Paine and Sam Adams had provided better revolutionary guides than either Marx or Lenin.

Some time during the sixties America discovered demography: a new world came into view, lying off the coast of California and containing almost everyone alive. The China Lobby alarmists were proved right; a Yellow Peril did indeed exist, but its true threat arose from masses of people multiplied into power, rather than from ideology. The highly touted American Century had lasted less than a decade, coinciding roughly with the Eisenhower era. The future would not be European, or American, or Russian. It would be primarily Oriental.

An overstatement? Yes. A caricature? Certainly. The West still has a slight basis for hope, for despite their official bravado at mass ceremonies, Orientals do not really believe in their own ascendency. Our technological and scientific lead-time, although diminishing, will still be a governing factor in the immediate future. The facts are obscured by the generalized neuralgic trauma anything communist produces in Americans, who are finding the Chinese strain even more terrifying than the Russian. Perversely, and with characteristic ineptitude, Americans managed to hound Owen Lattimore out of the country; he is one of the very few men alive with specialized knowledge of the Mongol borderland that both Russia and China covet. True, in recent months American Sinologists have started talking sense in public again, but more than a few television discussion programs will be required to make America change its mind about the Chinese Reds.

Past experience has demonstrated America's virtual inability to produce a rational policy in any realm of foreign affairs. The American party system subordinates the general interests of the American people to the particular interests of those localities and interest groups that control the grass roots of the party organizations. Political scientists have long bemoaned the fact that there is no "constituency" for foreign affairs in American politics; the interests of every locality are well represented when foreign policies are at issue, but the interests of the nation as a whole go unattended. In short, American politics reverses an elementary maxim of reason, and the sum of its parts is *greater* than the whole. Until American politics can extricate itself from this twisted logic, it can only spread unreason in the world.

Until about twenty years ago this malady produced only irrational tariff policies and short-sighted isolationism, but a change came after World War II. Then a positive constituency developed to exercise power in foreign affairs, and the force it represented *was* force. The late President Eisenhower presciently identified the new constituency as the military-industrial complex. It has its own foreign policy, and that is to treat any issue that might arise by means of armed force. Recently the military-industrial complex has joined hands with party hacks and pressure groups, and the American party system has acquired a built-in bias toward both unreason and war.

Gradually, almost imperceptibly at first, another equally informal new constituency has arisen in American politics: it might be called the black-youth-mandarin complex. Its methods may tend to violence, but it exerts a positive force for peace in foreign affairs. This inchoate coalition, espoused by such as Tom Hayden, Eldridge Cleaver, and Noam Chomsky, among others, has been able to unseat Lyndon Johnson, to shatter the Democratic Party in convention assembled, and to turn our universities into guerrilla outposts.

Today these new imperialists and new anti-imperialists are arrayed against each other in an undeclared war, as befits our times, for the control of America. This is the content of the "new politics." If, in Harry Ashmore's words, "we don't run out of era" too soon, the anti-imperialists will surely win, but this is precisely what is in doubt.

For roughly two decades following 1946, most nations seemed able to innoculate themselves moderately well against the endemic diseases of the American polity. The United States could play fast and loose with atomic diplomacy, containment, and brinksmanship; so long as Europe remained sane, Russia cautious, and China weak, it was impossible for America to push the world over the brink. Whom could Americans fight? Not the Russians, at least, not at first; that battle must be saved for the last. American armies, and later American industries, controlled all of Western Europe. Eastern Europe and Russia's borders were off-limits for fear of getting into that last big war too soon. Everywhere else the American establishment was free to play out war scenarios to its heart's delight: in Greece, the Middle East, Africa, Central America, the Caribbean, and Southeast Asia.

But then a group of upstarts began to close down the American playgrounds. The thermonuclear club grew to five, with several more impatient aspirants knocking at the door. The "Nth Country" problem even threatened to grow into the Nth factory problem; scientific journals told us uranium was plentiful enough for any bright tinkerer with access to a fairly good machine shop to put together an old-fashioned, Hiroshima-sized firecracker. Of course, obtaining delivery systems remained a problem, but with airfreight rates becoming more and more reasonable and with plane hi-jacking techniques well-perfected, PanAm, Flying Tiger, or almost any other line could easily be finessed into delivery service.

Richard Nixon, who had learned about politics from Allen and John Foster Dulles, came to office just as the postwar era of little wars—"brushfires" we dubbed them—was drawing to a close. Korea and Vietnam were hardly little, although officially one was only a police action and the other no war at all. Both of these non-wars were obviously directed against

China—the *Cordon Chinoise*—and this is certain to haunt what little era may be left to us.

Meanwhile, the American virus spread to Europe. England and France tried to emulate Dulles in the Suez. After Khrushchev the disease invaded Russia. The Brezhnev Doctrine that rationalized the liberation of Czechoslovakia from the grasp of her revisionist heretics was cribbed almost word for word from the Truman Doctrine. Neither European nor Russian rationality could be relied on any longer to counteract the gangland regime America was foisting on world politics.

Neo-Stalinism was not the culprit—quite the contrary. Stalin had been cautious to the point of timidity except for his sensitivity over the invasion routes to Russia. But out of the internal political disarray in post-Khrushchevian Russia there emerged a Soviet version of America's own military-industrial complex. This military-industrial complex conspired with Russia's local party cadres, who used pressure politics freely, to produce in Russia very nearly the same forces that had contorted American foreign policy for nearly a generation. At the same time, Russia began to feel the force of an embryonic internal opposition recruited from the young and the intellectuals, the latter symbolized by Solzhenitsyn and Sakarhov.

But what of the wily Chinese? Our Sinologists assure us that caution has always ruled their councils. Our psychologists and geneticists tell us that they are at least as bright, if not brighter, than the whites. Our historians tell us that, except for the century beginning around 1848, theirs had been the world's highest culture for many millenia. Perhaps, one could hope, *they* would be wise enough to inhibit the dedication to gangsterism characteristic of every other chancery. Unfortunately, China has now contracted the same disease that afflicts the others. In the wake of her Cultural Revolution, many of the same forces that rule Russia and America have come to the fore. The regional authorities that have succeeded her traditional provincial warlords are unable to produce a rational foreign policy in the general interests of the Chinese people. In concert with the military and industrial elites, they can find a consensus only for showing a belligerent face to the outside world.

Domestic distempers afflict all the lords of the earth. They can see no alternative but to gird themselves for a Götterdammerung.

None of this is secret. The hapless onlookers know it well. The Canadians see through the pious protestations of the Americans, the Czechs smile grimly and knowingly at the Russians, and the Japanese reflect sadly on the future prospect of a heavily Sionized Asia. Within each of the Big Three powers, opposition liberals steadily gain influence. Hans Bethe is echoed by Sakarhov, and we may be certain that their counterpart stands at the apex of Chinese science. Aiichiro Fujiyama and the opposition liberals of Japan hear their own voices echoed by the McCarthy-Kennedy-Fulbright opposition liberals in the United States Senate. In all these cases, the constituencies grow larger every day.

A new kind of international politics has begun to grow up inside the old. There is a bare chance—and this is the avowed aim of opposition liberals in Japan—that if liberals can form a transnational coalition dedicated to international sanity, the world might be returned to the right track. Even more important is the possibility that this coalition may provide support for their presently muzzled Russian and Chinese counterparts. Should an opposition liberal group come to power in any country, the internal position of the others would be greatly enhanced. An even more significant transnational foreign policy alliance might become feasible, and world politics would acquire an entirely new scope.

In former times nations played at balance-of-power politics in much the way that young boys play at marbles. Disagreement always ended in a scrap, and that settled things for a while. This was the game according to Clausewitz: war was the extension of diplomacy "by other means" and perfectly normal for old-style nation-states. But what happens when Clausewitz is vetoed by H-Bombs, which say that war can no longer be regarded as an instrument of foreign policy? The atom's first revised lesson of diplomacy is that only peripheral areas and only obscure states can still utilize war to settle their disputes, and these areas are fast diminishing.

Physicists tell us that soon not even Jews and Arabs will be able to keep at their old-fashioned war play, for each is about to demand admittance to the thermonuclear club. But conflicts, unaware of new rules, keep erupting as if Clausewitz were still the world's croupier. When these conflicts are as grave, or perhaps graver, than ever before, we find ourselves unable to apply the old rules of warfare. What now?

The world's response has been to develop a new form of balance-of-power politics, one attempting to disrupt the internal political processes of other countries instead of mobilizing for war against them. The Japanese, deprived for over a generation of recourse to the Old World's Clausewitzian rules, have become most adept at playing the game of world politics according to this new rule, and the rest of the world is rapidly learning.

Official American and Japanese policies toward China are war-prone, and, now that China has joined the thermonuclear club, irrational as well. At the same time the traditional alternative to war, diplomacy, is anathema to both American and Japanese military-industrialists. To achieve peaceful resolution of their mutual difficulties with China, both Japan and the United States need new rational leadership to displace the ruling military-industrial elite. The leadership potential exists in each country among minority opposition groups both within and outside the governments. The essence of the new balance-of-power politics is that liberals in one country can influence the *internal* factional struggle within every other country to inhibit the authority of militarists. In the absence of a workable world order, this mode of transnational political coöperation is the only alternative to thermonuclear war.

Enforced demilitarization induced Japan to learn this new mode of world politics many years ago, but Japan is no longer alone. Russian-American relations have alternated between old style belligerent threats and new style balance-of-power ploys. President Kennedy often pleaded for moderation from Congressional cold-warriors on the ground that America should do everything possible to support the Kremlin "doves" and discredit Kremlin "hawks." Khrushchev has stated that he played exactly the same role in the Kremlin and went so far as to claim credit for Kennedy's Presidential victory over Nixon. Despite Nixon's urgent pleas, the release of the downed Navy fliers was delayed by Khrushchev until after the American Presidential election. Khrushchev has explained that he believed Kennedy would be less belligerent than Nixon, and he designed Soviet policies toward America accordingly. The electoral outcome was so close that some credence must be given to Khrushchev's boast.

Current history offers many more illustrations of the new balance-of-power diplomacy. Hanoi makes its moves with one eye on the war front and the other on America's domestic opposition to that war. Indeed, the guiding maxim, understood by both sides, is that the defeat of the French occurred in Paris rather than Dien Bien Phu.

Today, even in war, the new diplomacy, rather than events on the battlefield, determines the outcome. This was the lesson of Korea. Game-theory militarists hailed that war as proof that non-nuclear conventional war could still be used to end international conflicts. Actually, it proved just the opposite. The Korean War ended nothing but the Democrats' lease on the White House. The conclusion must be that the new balance-of-power diplomacy actually works and is the only course that can work in foreign affairs today.

To most Americans, expanding economic and cultural relations with Peking, scuttling Chiang Kai-shek, and installing mainland China, Japan, and India as permanent members of the United Nations Security Council may seem far too visionary. But events move quickly under the new diplomacy. A year ago who would have predicted that prominent American conservatives would be advocating a Sino-American détente in order to embarrass Russia? Once the tide of events turns, changes and adjustments too long postponed may overwhelm America at a breathtaking pace.

Demographically, economically, and culturally the world is certain to acquire an Oriental cast in the future, a prospect perhaps as desirable as it is inevitable. The West has served nature and mankind ill during its short stewardship of history. The counsel of wisdom, for America as well as for the world, is to adjust as rapidly and as wisely as possible to the eventuality of an Asian world and to prepare now for ultimate acceptance as a minor partner in some future form of Asiatic union. This is the goal toward which our own new balance-of-power diplomacy should aim.

RECIPE FOR SURVIVAL:
AN UNTRIED APPROACH IN
AN UNPRECEDENTED AGE

WILLIAM O. DOUGLAS:

Every man, whatever his race or national origin, has a deep-seated instinct for survival; and the nuclear age underlines for all of us the increasing risks of turning our cities and factories into nuclear incinerators.

War today is too awful and too expensive to consider. In the old days a war could be a healthy thing; it could generate a good Churchillian feeling of strong men and proud women. But in the present the ancient solution of armed force applied to international disputes will eventually mean the destruction of all our great countries—the United States, China, Japan, and Russia; and it would spell the end of civilization as we know it. We have arrived at the end of the road as far as war is concerned.

The whole sweep of recorded history tells us graphically that preparedness and armaments races ultimately lead to war. There is no such thing as a deterrent power; there is no such thing as preparing against an aggressor. The more one nation arms, the more another follows suit. In the end, an evitable collision will bring us to the ultimate confrontation.

The search for alternatives must begin. The problem is not an easy one; solutions will not appear overnight. The world needs a new and wholly different approach, a fresh mood, so that the peoples on this planet can find in their common bond of humanity a rule for living to take the place of the rule of destruction and death.

In the nineteen-fifties the United States entered an era of political bankruptcy. Politicians aped the generals and admirals, and everyone in America became a military expert. Where should we put the Seventh Fleet, the Fifth Fleet, or the Sixth Fleet? The troops, the planes, the bases, and the missiles? By now America is spending two and a half billion dollars a month in Vietnam, and the budget for the Pentagon has reached eighty billion dollars this year.

Man is unruly; man is ambitious; man is greedy; man is overreaching. Nations are made up of men, and accidents happen.

Washington fears Peking; Tokyo is afraid of Moscow; and Russia and China hasten to arm against the West.

When, at the height of his power, Nikita Khrushchev suggested some elementary steps toward a new kind of world security, he was laughed off the front pages of American newspapers. Silly old Mr. Khrushchev! His ridiculous suggestion was that the nations of the world should try to agree upon the amicable settlement of boundary questions and territorial disputes—the beginning of a rule of law in world affairs. Silly old Mr. Khrushchev?

The time has come for Japan and Russia, and eventually China, to sit down with the United States to work out a consensus, to lay down the ground rules for settling international disputes. In America fifty sovereign states submit their conflicts to judicial arbitration without bloodshed. Why not in the world at large?

The countries of the world today need to establish specialized institutions through which many kinds of conflict can be channeled. When we realize that between 1917 and 1968 the United States worked out forty-seven treaties with Soviet Russia, twenty-five of them still in operation, we can understand that legal solutions to our conflicts are not entirely Utopian. How many nations today belong to the Postal Union? *Every one.* These were miniscule treaties aimed at tiny problems, but they contain the ingredients from which a coöperative world regime can one day develop. These little treaties form the first part of a great mosaic that will, if we try, culminate in a world rule of law.

Some machinery exists—the Commission on Human Rights and the International Court of Justice. From the days of John Foster Dulles, the jurisdiction of the International Court has been subject to American approval when the United States is being sued, the so-called Connally Amendment. Eighty-five nations followed the American lead, including the U.S.S.R. The views of John Foster Dulles and the politburo in Moscow are almost identical. When nations will not accept obligatory jurisdiction, they cannot enforce it on others. The International Court has never handled more than six cases in any one year. Last year it had one.

If there is to be a new age in Asia, Japan, China, and the United States must initially take the lead. Japan is not an American client state. Her achievements in education, science, technology, marketing, diplomacy, and law place her among the great powers. Since I started my Asian journeys twenty years ago, I have felt that of all the Asian nations Japan and India, once freed from American military excitement, could, with China, best produce a regime of law to supplant the present regime of force.

The starting point must be with Japan and the United States. Unilateral action is not the course. Japan and the United States need to reëvaluate the entire Asian scene, and each must decide what role to play in developing peaceful resolutions of rivalries and conflicts.

China is, of course, the exponent of a highly competitive ideology. Peking inspires many developing peoples or individuals seeking escape from some form of feudalism that entraps them. Once, the United States was also revolutionary in the sense that it inspired people to revolt. World problems are not soluble if every nation but one must surrender that role and agree not to excite revolution. Coexistence—indeed coevolution—is a necessary tenet of any new world order.

An autopsy of the old order is not helpful. The aim should be building coöperative Asian patterns whereby national boundaries are fixed and guaranteed, where trade and commerce are freely developed, where diplomacy holds sway, and where international tribunals or agencies are created to arbitrate, compromise, or adjudicate conflicting claims among nations.

Asia, dominated by Japan, India, and China, can easily lead the world in showing how a regional regime of the rule of law can flourish.

APPENDIX I

TERRITORIES CLAIMED BY
THE PEOPLE'S REPUBLIC OF CHINA
AS HISTORICALLY SUBJECT TO CHINESE SUZERAINTY

DATE ACQUIRED	AREA IN SQUARE KILO-METERS	LOCATION	NEW OWNER-SHIP
1689	240,000	North side Khingan Mountains	Russia
1727	100,000	Lower Selenga Valley	Russia
1842	83	Hong Kong	U.K.
1858	480,000	North of Heilungkiang	Russia
1858	8	Kowloon	U.K.
1860	344,000	East of Ussuri River	Russia
1864	900,000	North of Balkhash	Russia
1879	2,386	Liuchiu Islands	Japan
1882-1883	21,000	Lower Lli Valley	Russia
1883	20,000	Irtysh Valley east of Lake Zansan	Russia
1884	9,000	Upper Koksol Valley	Russia
1885-1889	738,000	Annam and all Indochina	France
1886	574,000	Burma	U.K.
1890	7,550	Sikkim	U.K.
1894	122,400	West of the upper Salween	U.K.
1894	91,300	West of the upper Yangtze	U.K.
1894	100,000	Upper Burma, Savage Mountains	U.K.
1895	220,334	Korea	Japan
1895	35,845	Taiwan	Japan
1895	127	Pescadores	Japan
1897	760	The edge of Burma	U.K.
1897	2,300	The edge of Burma	U.K.
Total:	4,009,093		

From Allen S. Whiting, "Foreign Policy of Communist China," *Foreign Policy in World Politics,* Roy C. Macridis, ed. Prentice-Hall: 1967

APPENDIX II

A TABULATION OF THE VOTES IN THE
UNITED NATIONS GENERAL ASSEMBLY
ON THE ADMITTANCE OF CHINA

PREPARED BY Aiichiro Fujiyama

On the Question of Considering the Representation of Mainland China:
The Moratorium Formula

GENERAL ASSEMBLY	FOR	AGAINST	ABSTAIN
6th, 1951	37	11	4
7th, 1952	42	7	11
8th, 1953	44	10	2
9th, 1954	43	11	6
10th, 1955	42	12	6
11th, 1956	47	24	8
12th, 1957	48	27	6
13th, 1958	44	28	9
14th, 1959	44	29	9
15th, 1960	42	34	22

On the Important Question Resolution and the Albanian Resolution

GENERAL ASSEMBLY	(*Albanian*)			(*Important Question*)		
	FOR	AGAINST	ABSTAIN	FOR	AGAINST	ABSTAIN
16th, 1961	36	48	20	61	34	7
17th, 1962	42	56	12			
18th, 1963	41	57	12			
20th, 1965	47	47	20	56	49	11
21st, 1966	46	57	17	66	48	7
22nd, 1967	45	58	17	69	48	4
23rd, 1968	44	58	23	73	47	5

APPENDIX III

RESULTS OF A POLL OF MEMBERS OF THE UNITED STATES HOUSE OF REPRESENTATIVES ON QUESTIONS OF CHINA POLICY

Taken in December, 1968 by Don Edwards, Member of Congress
Ninety Replies Received

1 If Japan should decide to initiate full trade, travel, and political relations with mainland China, would you be:

Openly critical	25%
Quietly critical	25%
Pleased publicly	20%
Pleased privately	14%
Neutral	16%

2 If you made a public statement suggesting that the United States have trade, travel and political relations with China, including recognition and U.N. membership, what would be the reaction of your constituents?

Adverse	76%
Favorable	10%
Divided	14%

3   Should President Nixon announce recognition of mainland China and his decision to support her admission to the U.N., would you be:

Openly critical	35%
Quietly critical	17%
Pleased publicly	32%
Pleased privately	7%
Neutral	9%

4   Do you think that Japan should have a substantial military responsibility in the Far East?

Yes	79%
No	21%

5   If your answer to question four is yes, would you favor nuclear arms for Japan?

Yes	14%
No	86%

6   Remarks:

"I believe that improved relations between the United States and China will serve the long-range interests of the United States and the cause of world peace. However, any move in that direction on our part should not be taken in the absence of some genuine and concrete moves on the part of China to cease hostile action against the United States and the free world and to indicate a willingness to become a responsible member of the family of nations and to honor international agreements."

"Japan needs assurance that our willingness to defend her is absolute. If she has this assurance, she won't need nuclear arms nor will she feel need for them. However, if we waver, then Japan will logically do what is necessary for her security."

234

"I am opposed to trade with any of the 'unfriendly countries' and am opposed to the admission of Red China to the United Nations."

"I have been to Japan and have a great respect for the Japanese and their order in society. Yet, I can never forget their desire for world superiority, and am skeptical of giving them any U.S. endorsement that could be interpreted as our surrender in Asia and that might reinstitute the Japanese culture as the wave of the future.
"The graves of far too many of our comrades are too fresh to forget the hard lesson that should have been learned in the epic battles of cultural wars."

"No real balance will be achieved in the Orient until Japan assumes a political role commensurate with the economic power she now wields. Japan should assume more of her own defense. She is the perfect balance to China. This line should have been adopted by the United States ten years ago. Our own relationship with China can be settled, in my opinion, only when Mao is dead and new leadership is willing to recognize the status quo. Then I would favor recognition."

"I would be critical only of a recognition and support for admission that implied no thought of reciprocity from China in the form of adherence to the principles of the U.N. Charter or the admission of Western journalists to China, cultural exchange, and the like."

"More Japanese-Chinese trade may be inevitable and in the long run perhaps not entirely bad. Arming Japan also has its dangers, but it too seems inevitable and logical, and we must keep her friendly.
"I am opposed to recognition and admission of Red China now or in the foreseeable future, and I am sure my constituents would oppose it."

"I'm in favor of diplomatic normalcy with Peking, but I doubt that Red China's terms would be acceptable."

"I think it imperative that we permit Japan to have a large standing army."

"I think China should be admitted to the United Nations, but not ro replace Formosa and, in view of her present attitudes, without a veto on the Security Council.
"I think there should be a quid pro quo of non-militarism and release of prisoners exacted for recognition. Trade, cultural relations, and so forth should be a two-way street."

"A growing Asian economic and defense community anchored in Japan, India and Indonesia, with U.S. backing, would reduce the need for standing U.S. deployments in the Far East and make possible true neutralization of certain friction points, such as Vietnam, Laos, Cambodia, and Burma. A major U.S. effort should be made to replace the Okinawa base, even at considerable expense, and promptly guarantee Okinawa's return to Japan in five to seven years."

"Recognition of mainland China and her admission to the United Nations must be predicated upon her solemn pledge to give up her imperialistic ideology and her public demonstration of the intention to live peacefully with her neighbors. Otherwise she remains an outlaw in the family of nations."

"American foreign policy toward Red China should be to fragment her, that is, to encourage every divisive trend, rather than to accord her any respectability or legitimacy."

"Until the People's Republic of China convinces me that she is ready to accept the responsibilities of world integration. I cannot support a movement to give her the prestige and economic uplift she would receive from recognition by our government.

"While our current policy cannot realistically be maintained indefinitely, we do not need to move now to enhance China's entry into the world marketplace nor the world's diplomatic forums. However, it is my view that the very chance that we may do so is a good leverage to use with the U.S.S.R. in forcing them to join with us in insuring a more stable atmosphere for peace—not only in Asia and the Middle East but elsewhere. The threat of our opening better relations with China could make Russian policies improve.

"I do not, in regard to Japan, regard her role as one that should encompass nuclear armaments. However, she should definitely build for conventional wars, and, while she probably never will have to engage in them, it would prove a very stabilizing influence in Asian affairs if she had military power to equal her growing industrial might.

"I would vocally and actively oppose opening new ties with the People's Republic of China at this time."

ACKNOWLEDGEMENTS

The Center for the Study of Democratic Institutions wishes to express its gratitude to MR. PETER SHINO- BU HIGASHI and the corps of translators who accompanied him to Santa Barbara for the Japanese-American Conference on China Policy. Mr. Higashi, a veteran interpreter as well as Assistant Chief of Bureau for the Associated Press in Tokyo, took a leave of absence from his journalistic duties to come to Santa Barbara. With him were MR. HIROSHI DAY INOSHITA, a graduate of the University of California at Los Angeles and now a journalist, who has served as a simultaneous interpreter at many international conferences; MR. MASUMI MURAMATSU, who attended Waseda University in Tokyo and George Washington University in Washington, D.C., and is Executive Director of both Simul International, Inc. and Simul Press, Inc., and MRS. HIROKO NAGAMATSU, who received a degree in linguistics from International Christian University in Tokyo and has since acted as a simultaneous and consecutive interpreter at international conferences both at home and abroad. Without their professional assistance, the informal exchange of ideas that gave value to the discussions at the Center would not have been possible.

The Center also acknowledges contributions from the NEW POLICY DISCUSSION GROUP of the Liberal Democratic Party of Japan and from MR. MARTIN STONE of Los Angeles, which helped to finance the conference.

Photographs are by Leinie Schilling Nagel, Jimmy Chen, and Bill Bridges; book design by Lauri Provencher.

238

A8275